RISKING
THE
TRUTH

What a novel way to approach this most vital of subjects! Given that theological reflection is human thought about the Scriptural revelation of a tri-personal God, I have always believed that the personal element has a place in all of our theologizing. The subjective should not – indeed cannot – be removed from theology. And here we see the way that some of the most important theological minds of our day personally grapple with how truth is to be defended. This mesh of subjectivity and Christian apologetics – in which objectivity is so vital – makes for both compelling and profoundly instructive reading.

Michael A.G. Haykin,
Professor of Church History and Biblical Spirituality,
The Southern Baptist Theological Seminary, Louisville, Kentucky

Serious. Thoughtful. Humble. Godly. Loving. Bracing. Encouraging. These interviews will be a blessing to anyone seeking to be faithful in Christian ministry.

James M. Hamilton Jr.,
Associate Professor of Biblical Theology,
The Southern Baptist Theological Seminary, Louisville, Kentucky

This collection is fascinating, sobering and encouraging. It presents an impressive range of experience and wisdom on the challenges facing the church and its ministry in dealing with false teaching while being sensitive to those affected by it.

Robert Letham,
Full-time Lecturer,
Wales Evangelical School of Theology

This is a book that promotes reflection. By introducing you to a number of leading Christian thinkers, it gives you a read that is interesting, informative and stimulating. It provides you with a treasure-chest of historical, theological and practical insights as it airs issues that are confronting the worldwide church and its leaders at the present time. Christian pastors, leaders and academics who neglect this book will be very much the poorer intellectually, spiritually and practically.

Stuart Olyott,
Pastoral Director,
Evangelical Movement of Wales

RISKING
THE
TRUTH

Interviews on Handling
Truth and
Error in the Church

MARTIN DOWNES

Martin Downes is minister of Christ Church Deeside in North Wales. Prior to that he worked in student ministry. He has written several magazine and journal articles and contributed to *Reforming or Conforming?* (Crossway) and *Keeping Your Balance* (IVP:Apollos).

Copyright© Martin Downes

ISBN 978-1-84550-284-3

10 9 8 7 6 5 4 3 2 1

Printed 2009
by
Christian Focus Publications Ltd.,
Geanies House, Fearn, Ross-shire,
IV20 1TW, Scotland, Great Britain

www.christianfocus.com

Cover design by Moose77.com
Printed by Bell and Bain, Ltd., Glasgow

Mixed Sources
Product group from well-managed forests and other controlled sources
www.fsc.org Cert no.TT-COC-002769
© 1996 Forest Stewardship Council
FSC

Contents

DEDICATION

For my wife, Debbie

Proverbs 31:10-11, 29

FOREWORD

It is a privilege to introduce and recommend this unique book. The brain-child of Martin Downes it makes a very distinctive contribution to the early twenty-first century church. In addition, for anyone interested in the views of some of the thought-leaders in a variety of reformed communities, Martin Downes has assembled an all-star team whose contexts are as diverse as – among other places – the Western Isles of Scotland where Iain D Campbell is minister, to the Eastern States of the USA where Carl Trueman and Mark Dever reside, Wheaton outside of Chicago where Greg Beale teaches, Jackson, Mississippi (which wins the prize for its three resident contributors), to the West Coast of America, and then to Africa where Conrad Mbewe serves as pastor of Kabwata Baptist Church in Zambia, and then to London where Mike Ovey teaches theology, and back to home base in Wales where Martin Downes himself is a minister.

These are men to whom others, older as well as younger, look to guide their patterns of thought about the gospel, the church and the world. Most of them know each other personally, or at least by reputation, and share a mutual esteem for one another's work. In addition, they all belong to a variety of 'communities' connected together in an unplanned but real network of churches, institutions and publications. Together they represent a prodigious literary output.

These 'communities' – churches, seminaries, organizations and informal networks – share in different ways in the extraordinary world-wide resurgence of reformed theology that has taken place in the past half century or so. Some of them are part of denominations (such as The Free Church of Scotland) or institutions (like Westminster Theological Seminary) which have long maintained the theology of Calvin and the Reformed Confessions. But others – as their personal testimonies indicate – have, with a multitude of others, come upon reformed theology only by experiencing what Calvin himself described as an 'unexpected conversion'.

Most of these men belong to the second and third generations of this resurgence and are now engaged in significant ministries that seek to encourage and train the fourth generation. Perhaps this fourth generation will prove to be the most interesting and widespread generation yet. For fascinatingly, while in the 1960s 'The Jesus Movement' might be mentioned in secular publications such as *Time* magazine, in that magazine's 2009 annual review of ideas that are changing the world, the new Calvinism was listed as number three.

In many ways this is a sign of both growth and decay. It signals remarkable growth in the influence of reformed theology. Many are turning to it having found that much generic evangelicalism has drifted at one edge into superficiality and at the other into theological convictions antithetical to the fundamentally reformed orientation of classical evangelicalism. Today – not least among younger men and women – the importance of doctrine, seriousness of spirituality, and a recovery of biblical exposition, have all become major *desiderata* in the movements with which they want to be identified.

Over the centuries when God has purposed a fresh work he has often brought together brotherhoods or networks of Christian leaders to point the way forwards. This is in some measure happening in our own day. To use the language of 2 Samuel 5:24, there is 'the sound of marching in the tops of the balsam trees ...' and a sense that 'the Lord has gone out before you'.

It is, therefore, an exciting time to be reformed.

But exciting times can also be testing times. New energy and zeal are often accompanied by short roots that do not go down deeply into the soil. The discovery of new doctrine can easily lead to imbalance. It can propel an individual into an unhealthy desire always to hold something new. But the highway to novelty is also the road to deviation.

Against that background Martin Downes has asked each of these interviewees a series of penetrating questions about false teaching and living – how it arises, why we fall into it, what contributes to it, and how in distinction we can maintain faithfulness to the gospel. The fact that we have twenty of them is itself a safeguard against the ever-present danger of 'choose your guru'. For here we find diversity of personality (the interviewees are far from being a collection of cookie-cutter clones!). Variety of context and personal background guarantees a healthy diversity of approach. There is safety in a community of counselors.

Yet at the same time, running throughout these pages is a strong consistency. Things may be said in different words, but the same emphases recur again and again. Among these emphases are: the importance of biblical exposition in the life of the church, the value of the well-tested and pastorally well-proven Confessions of the church, the importance of guarding the heart, the privilege of genuine friendships in which men seek to hold each other to a gospel life-style.

So, put some logs, or coal, or peat, on the fire; make (or fix) yourself a pot of tea or coffee; settle back into your favorite chair – and spend an evening or a rainy afternoon in the company of Martin Downes. Enjoy the way in which he brings one after another of these thought-leaders into your living room – and then himself sits down to talk with you before the end of the day. Here you will find food for thought, and much to bring practical stimulus and challenge. And you will surely be the better for it. I hope I am.

Sinclair B Ferguson
First Presbyterian Church, Columbia, South Carolina

TAKING ERROR
WITH
APOSTOLIC SERIOUSNESS

Every generation of the church needs to cultivate doctrinal discernment with regard to truth and error. Every generation of church leaders need to practice pastoral vigilance in the nurture and protection of the flock. God's Word on these matters must be understood and applied.

In this regard there are unchanging positive calls to preach the Word (2 Tim. 4:1-2), to teach the whole counsel of God (Acts 20:27), to hold fast to the gospel (1 Cor. 15:1-2), to follow the pattern of sound words (2 Tim. 1:13; 1 Tim. 4:6), to guard the good deposit (2 Tim. 1:14; 1 Tim. 6:20), to appoint faithful men able to teach others also (2 Tim. 2:2), and to teach disciples all that Jesus has commanded them to obey (Matt. 28:19-20). These imperatives set the tone and direction of Christian ministry. They call for a wholehearted commitment to love the Lord our God, to be faithful stewards of the gospel, and to feed His sheep (Jer. 3:15; 1 Cor. 4:1-2; Titus 1:9; 1 Pet. 5:2).

Alongside these positive calls are the unrelenting warnings about the presence of false teachers, and clear instructions about how to deal with them (Rom. 16:17-18; Eph. 4:14; 1 Tim. 1:3-4; 2 Tim. 2:16, 22-26; Titus 1:11; 3:9-11; 2 Pet. 2:1-3). These warnings are clothed in powerful images. False teachers are wolves, dogs, waterless clouds, fruitless trees, wild waves, wandering stars, and their teaching will eat up like gangrene (Matt. 7:15-20; Acts 20:29; Phil. 3:2; 2 Tim. 2:17; Jude 12-13).

It is required of church leaders that they keep a watch on themselves, their teaching, and the flock entrusted to their care (Acts 20:28, 31; 1 Tim. 4:16). They must have a solid grasp of sound doctrine, held with a clear conscience, and an ability to mix it with false teachers (1 Tim. 1:5, 19; Titus 1:9). Truth must be taught and those in error must be rebuked and their teaching refuted.

Scripture never soft pedals the true nature and effects of heresy. It regards the most virulent forms of error as soul destroying and insidiously evil (Gal. 1:6-9; 2 Cor. 11:1-4, 12-15; 1 Tim. 4:1-3; 2 Tim. 2:25-26; 1 John 2:22; 4:3; 2 John 7). Harold O. J. Brown underlined the seriousness of rejecting the true gospel and embracing a different one:

> ...just as there are doctrines that are true, and that can bring salvation, there are those that are false, so false that they can spell eternal damnation for those who have the misfortune to be entrapped by them.

Nevertheless, in God's providence, these errors have been the occasion of producing greater clarity in the articulation of the essential articles of the Christian faith. They have also provoked some of the most substantial responses to be found in the theological literature of the Church. Alfred North Whitehead, of all people, rightly remarked that 'wherever there is a creed, there is a heretic round the corner or in his grave.' Rather more positively, Martin Luther was right to say that 'If heresies and offenses come, Christendom will only profit thereby, for they make Christians to read diligently facing evangelicals today. We will be all the poorer if we neglect the great ecumenical creeds of the early church, the weighty confessions of the Reformation, and the legacies of the giants of Church history.

There are real spiritual dangers that face us when we think about errors, heresies and false teaching. On the one hand there is a temptation to fixate upon them, to become preoccupied, and to be sidetracked from following the pattern of apostolic ministry. On the other hand it is all too easy, especially in a cultural atmosphere of tolerance, to treat soul destroying error with complacency. There are dangers to the objective content of our faith, and to the subjective shape and health of our faith.

Preoccupation with error can blind us to the presence of pride. Schaeffer warned against this in *The Great Evangelical Disaster*:

> Thus whenever it becomes necessary to draw a line in the defense of a central Christian truth it is so easy to be proud, to be hard. It is easy to be self-righteous and to self- righteously think that we are so right on this one point that anything else may be excused – this is very easy, a very easy thing to fall into. These mistakes were indeed made, and we have suffered from this and the cause of Christ has suffered from this through some fifty years.

However, tolerance of error will inflict terrible damage to churches and to the cause of the gospel. Wayne Grudem has drawn attention to this with some quite sobering words in his contribution to *Beyond the Bounds*:

After reading such verses (2 Pet. 2:1; Jude 3-4), we might wonder if any of us have the same kind of heart for purity of doctrine in our Christian organizations, and the same sort of sober apprehension of the destructiveness of false doctrine, that the New Testament apostles had in their hearts. If we ever begin to doubt that false teaching is harmful to the church, or if we begin to become complacent about false doctrine, thinking that it is fascinating to ponder, stimulating to our thoughts, and worthwhile for discussion, then we should remind ourselves that in several cases the New Testament specifies that the ultimate source of many false teachings is Satan and his demons.

As a consequence these interviews are meant not only to inform us about error but to encourage God-honoring responses in how we handle it. Furthermore they will help us to consider how we handle our own hearts in doing so. There is a unified stress here on orthodoxy and orthopraxy.

What kind of doctrine is taught matters a great deal. On of the saddest things about evangelicalism today is the general aversion that exists toward doctrine. I generalize of course, and thankfully there is plenty of evidence to the contrary. Perhaps it is worth adding that the word 'doctrine' itself sends wrong signals when similar words do not. Doctrine is of course 'teaching', and Christian doctrine, as Jaroslav Pelikan put it, is 'what the church of Jesus Christ believes, teaches, and confesses on the basis of the Word of God.'

It is a mistake to think that theology and doctrine are confined to certain forms of literature, to specific environments, or that they should only be of interest to eggheads. Of course you can read about doctrine in hefty and imposing tomes, and you hear about it in academic lectures and debates. But you hear the same teachings in prayer, praise, and evangelism. Doctrine is found in the anguished confession of sin, and thank God, it is found in the sweet assurance of faith resting on the finished work of Christ. It is true doctrine that brings hope to sinners who turn to Christ, speaks peace to the guilty, gives direction to the wayward, and offers comfort to the grieving and to the dying. Strip away sound doctrine and all of these acts of faith and piety become empty, vague, and even perverse.

What makes biblical doctrine glorious is that it comes from the Triune God. And it is supremely about the Triune God. It is His own words about His work, His mighty acts of creation, providence and redemption. Without doctrine what grasp would we have of these things? How could we call on Him? How could we sing His praises? On what terms would we think that He accepts us? Doctrine is vital. It is simply essential.

Several of these interviews first appeared on the internet. The idea of turning them into a book I owe to one of the contributors, Geoffrey Thomas. It has been a great privilege to conduct these interviews, and I have gained more than I can adequately express in words from their seasoned wisdom. As the project got under way I was grateful for the help of my friend Daniel Strange, and for the wise advice of Scott Clark and Derek Thomas. I am also thankful too for the help of Willie MacKenzie and the staff at Christian Focus. Likewise I am thankful for the members and officers of Christ Church Deeside in North Wales whom it has been my great privilege to serve since August 2005. Due to a broken wrist I could not have completed the interviews and made it to the finishing line without the help of Rebecca Conway and Phil Greenow. Finally, and most importantly, I want to thank my wife Debbie, and our daughters Lowri and Kezia, for all their encouragement, love, and support.

Before turning to the interviews I want to put down in words a prayer for the author, contributors and readers alike:

> O Lord our God and Father, please look upon us in mercy and grace, please keep us from the sin of idolatry.
>
> O Lord, grant that we would always be satisfied with your truth, and submissive to your Word whatever the cost. Thank you that by your Spirit you have given us your Word, and by the Spirit's power have opened our eyes to believe and understand your Word.

Keep us from the wilful pride that would place your Word beneath the authority of our own thoughts and wisdom. Lord in your perfect and infinite wisdom you have permitted your Church to be in danger of deception to test the hearts of your people to see if they love you.

Keep us O Lord from abandoning your gospel, and from turning aside to that which is no gospel at all.

And may your Church submit to the teaching of your Word and not to the thoughts of men, the ways of the world, or the dressed up lies of the evil one. For the sake of the glory of your Son, without the true knowledge of whom no man may know you. Amen

CHAPTER ONE

HERESY 101

What do you associate that word with? Torches and pitchforks? Burning someone at the stake? The incessant barking of theological watchdogs? 'Health and wealth' preachers? Unbelieving bishops who deny the gospel but stay on the payroll of the church?

What is heresy?
One writer defines it as 'any teaching that directly contradicts the clear and direct witness of the Scriptures on a point of salvific importance.' Heresy is the kind of doctrinal error that is so serious that it redefines the gospel. Error is always costly. It dishonors God and damages the Church. But not all errors are heresies. A heretic is not someone who fails to explain adequately the doctrine of the Trinity, or that Jesus is both fully God and fully man, the nature of the atonement, or justification by faith alone. No, a heretic *denies* these truths and is fundamentally *unsubmissive* to apostolic doctrine and authority as it is given in Scripture.

Heresy is not a matter of opinion. We have an objective standard when we want to find out which theological view is correct or orthodox (meaning 'right belief'), as Paul shows in 1 Corinthians 15, and which ones are wrong. In the end the fight against heresy is always won by the clear, patient, and thorough exposition of Scripture. Perversely, successful heretics themselves often claim to be truly orthodox and biblical.

Heresy is, however, a matter of choice. It is the choice to believe a different gospel. Augustine said that heretics are men 'who were altogether broken off and alienated in matters relating to the actual faith.'

A heretic chooses to tell lies about the God of the Bible because he doesn't want to tell the truth. And a heretic is someone who refuses admonition and is divisive (Titus 3:10-11). Putting it mathematically, heretics *take away* from the truth of the gospel (and *adding* to the truth always takes away from it), they *divide* true churches and aim to *multiply* new disciples.

Where do heresies come from?

It is vitally important to realize that heresies do not originate in the minds of men and women. Ultimately heresy originates with the devil. When the apostle Paul takes the Corinthian church to task for tolerating false teachers he compares their approach to the deception of Eve by the serpent (2 Cor. 11:3). But the deception in the Garden is more than a useful illustration. The super-apostles at Corinth *are* the servants of the devil disguising themselves as apostles of Christ.

Similarly Paul warned Timothy about 'deceitful spirits and the teachings of demons' (1 Tim. 4:1), and of false teachers who are caught in the snare of the devil (2 Tim. 2:24-25). After all the devil is the father of lies (John 8:44). The connection between other Gospels and the demonic, which is integral to a biblical world-view, has been largely lost. If it were regained it would keep us from ever thinking that heresies are interesting, intellectually stimulating, tolerable, or in any way benign. Cyprian of Carthage, in the third century, made this insightful comment about heresy and the devil:

> There is more need to fear and beware of the Enemy when he creeps up secretly, when he beguiles us by a show of peace and steals forward by those hidden approaches which have earned him the name of the 'Serpent' ... He invented heresies and schisms so as to undermine the faith, to corrupt the truth, to sunder our unity. Those whom he failed to keep in the blindness of their old ways he beguiles, and leads them up a new road of illusion.

Or as the late Jaroslav Pelikan put it '*renouncing* the devil means *denouncing* heresy.'

Furthermore, it is vitally important to understand that heresy is the takeover of Christianity by an alien world-view. Paul warned the Colossians about 'plausible arguments' and those who were trying to take them captive by 'philosophy and empty deceit according to human tradition,' (Col. 2:4, 8). Heretics often use the words of the Bible, change their meaning, and hide false ideas under them. The label may still say 'Christ', 'salvation', or 'atonement' but the meanings of these words have been radically altered. The early church fathers were alert to this danger. They wrote books to expose the fact that heretics were really saying the same thing as pagan philosophers, only the heretics were dressing up these ideas in Christian language. This deceitfulness makes heresy morally as well as doctrinally wrong.

Why would anyone embrace heresy?

You would think that someone would have to be out of their right mind to believe heresy. Who, after all, wants to believe something that isn't true? But, to quote Lucifer in Milton's *Paradise Lost*, the anthem of heresy is that 'it is better to reign in hell than serve in heaven.' Every heresy appeals to our sinful wishes and desires, the 'way that we want things to be' and not the way that God has provided in the gospel, 'which is infinitely better for us' as Bishop Allison put it. Consider all the major heresies and you will find that they appeal, directly or indirectly, to our sinful reason, affections and will. Heresy *appears* to be beneficial, posing as good news and proclaiming Jesus (2 Cor. 11:4), but in *reality* like gangrene it destroys spiritual life (2 Tim. 2:17).

Heresy always presents itself as an improvement on the biblical gospel. For the Colossians it promised to overcome their struggle with sin and bring them closer to God. For the Galatians it would keep them from persecution and fuel their desire to justify themselves before God by their works.

Heresy never appears in its true colors. In his monumental work *Against Heresies* Irenaeus wrote that 'error, indeed, is never set forth in its naked deformity, lest, being thus exposed, it should at once be detected. But it is craftily decked out in an attractive dress, so as, by its outward form, to make it appear to the inexperienced (ridiculous as the expression may seem) *more true than the truth itself.*'

What are the effects of heresy?

Heresy brings confusion for unbelievers since they hear several different and contradictory voices all claiming to be telling them the authentic good news.

Heresy also brings trouble for the Church. Unless false teachers are silenced, as Paul tells Titus that they should be, they will ruin households and upset the faith of some (Titus 1:11). Genuine believers can be unsettled by the teaching of these men (2 Tim. 2:18). In addition to this damage, false teachers also drain the time, energy, and resources of churches when they are not dealt with. Drawn-out conflicts with false teachers can divert and distract gospel churches from evangelism and the planting and nurturing of new congregations.

Heresy places those who embrace it, and refuse to be corrected, in danger of eternal condemnation. At the very least the salvation of those who are deceived by gospel-denying error cannot be affirmed. There is hope that God may grant such people repentance. But the apostles did not shrink from spelling out the danger of turning to a 'different gospel.' Paul makes it clear that whether the 'false brothers', an angel from heaven, or *even the apostles themselves* preached another gospel than the one that Paul had preached then they should be accursed (Gal. 1:6-9).

Harold Brown summed up the consequences of truth and error by saying that 'just as there are doctrines that are true, and that can bring salvation, there are those that are false, so false that they can spell eternal damnation for those who have the misfortune to be entrapped by them.'

Why do heresies persist?

Church history tells the story of the battle between truth and error. Heresies arise, gain a following, are opposed and refuted from Scripture, and then the Church moves on and advances in the truth. Because of this we have great statements like the Nicene Creed and the Definition of Chalcedon. But if these errors have been dealt with in the past why do they come back again and again? Why do people today believe old heresies? There are three reasons:

1. The devil still deceives people into believing heresies by using human instruments to promote attractive and plausible teaching. He will continue to do this until Christ returns in glory.

2. The warnings and lessons from history are ignored or unknown. If we are ignorant of the past we will fail to see that heresies that today appear new, innovative and interesting are as old as dirt. Many of the errors finding a home in evangelicalism today were tried and found wanting by our great-great-grandfathers in the faith at the bar of Scripture.

3. Throughout history those who deny the truth and choose a different gospel are limited in the options available to them. In his study of heresies Harold Brown concluded that 'over and over again, in widely separated cultures, in different centuries, the same basic misunderstandings and misinterpretations of the person and work of Christ and His message reappear. *The persistence of the same stimulus, so to speak, repeatedly produces the same or similar reactions.*'

CHAPTER TWO

SIN
IN HIGH PLACES

An Interview with Carl R. Trueman

Carl R. Trueman is Professor of Historical Theology and Church History at Westminster Theological Seminary, Philadelphia, Pennsylvania. He is the author of *The Wages of Spin, Minority Report*, and *John Owen: Reformed Catholic, Renaissance Man*.

MARTIN DOWNES: As you reflect back on your student years and involvement in conservative evangelical organizations in the UK, were there men who started out with evangelical convictions who later moved away from the gospel? How did you cope with that?

CARL R. TRUEMAN: I always find it hard to speak or to write about such things. It is sad to see friends fall. Of course, I have known a few such figures; and, Martin, we have both worked together enough in the past to share a number of friends who are now nowhere in terms of orthodoxy and their Christian walk. In my experience, such friends and acquaintances have fallen into two broad categories. There are those who fell into serious immorality, homosexuality, adultery, bitterness of spirit, etc., and whose views seemed to shift almost as a result of the practical moral move, a way of getting out from under the demands of truth. Then there are a few who really do seem to be driven by intellectual crises and problems.

How have I coped? The fall of a friend or a respected mentor is hard to stomach; but there are a number of things which help us to understand these tragedies. I have a high view of human sin. I know that, left to themselves and placed in the perfect storm of circumstances, anyone is capable of anything. Remembering this basic fact means that, though we can be disappointed and surprised by individual falls, we should not see them as failures of the gospel but failures of sinful human nature. It is what I jokingly call Zen-Calvinism: once you are enlightened about and understand the universal power of sin, you can never be wrong-footed by the fall of another. Further, it should also prevent us from standing in pharisaic judgment on such friends. Sin needs rebuking and, if necessary, church discipline; but we do this in a spirit of love to God and out of a desire to see the fallen one restored.

I must say, I do feel great personal sadness and some responsibility when I think of particular friends who have fallen and not, so far, returned to the church. It is always sobering to ask ourselves if we have failed as Christian friends in such circumstances: could we have been more available? Should we have intervened at an earlier stage when we saw the start of a self-destructive path? Why were we not the kind of people to whom our friends were able to turn with their struggles and doubts? Did we preach the gospel to our friends as we should have done? There are names I won't mention of friends who have fallen and who will always lie somewhat heavy on my conscience. Of course, everyone must take responsibility for their own actions and thoughts, but such questions are helpful in preventing self-righteous smugness relative to the failings of others.

DOWNES: Have you ever been drawn toward any views or movements that time has shown to have been unhelpful or even dangerous theologically?

TRUEMAN: I dallied briefly with Barthianism and then with Berkouwer's theology in the late 1980s. Studying at the University of Aberdeen, I found the dominant theology to be Barthianism refracted through the writings of the Torrance brothers. Berkouwer's *The Triumph of Grace in the Theology of Karl Barth* was helpful in giving me a critical handle on Barth and helping to free me from that particular dead-end; and his *Studies in Dogmatics* also gave me an appreciation for doing theology in a self-consciously historical manner. However, as my knowledge of confessional Reformed Orthodoxy developed in the early 1990s, through reading widely in the primary texts and the relevant secondary literature, and as I came to grips with the wider sweep of Western theology as I had to teach courses on medieval thought and on Thomas Aquinas at the University of Nottingham, I began to see how Berkouwer too had absorbed a lot of Barth and how this distorted his reception of theological tradition. At that point, I started to develop a much more carefully worked out confessional theology.

In practice, the theologies of Barth and Berkouwer have really proved sterile as ecclesiastical programs. The best one can say is that they failed to stop the collapse of vital church life in Scotland, Germany, Switzerland, and the Netherlands. For all of their criticisms of the 'static' God of orthodoxy, Barthian preaching is, in my experience, sterile and dull, and fails miserably to confront listeners with the God of the Bible. I personally know of no church which has really grown through Barthian preaching.

So I would summarize by saying that I am very grateful to Barth and Berkouwer for directing me to serious dogmatics, for fuelling my interest in theology and doctrinal history, and for raising big and important questions in my mind; and

I still enjoy reading them on occasion for the tremendous intellectual stimulation and challenge they provide; but I have ultimately found little of any real use, theological or practical, in the actual content of their theologies.

DOWNES: How should a minister keep his heart, mind and will from theological error?

TRUEMAN: No magic bullet here. The minister needs a good theological education, and then needs to maintain the basic disciplines of the Christian life – prayer and Bible reading, love to God and to neighbor. Of course, the minister does not sit under the preaching of the Word week by week, so accountability is even more of a problem for him than for others in the congregation. Presbyterianism has a structure of ministerial accountability in its church courts, but these are often impersonal and rather procedural gatherings. Even the Presbyterian minister still needs to make himself self-consciously accountable to others, a small group of one or more intimates.

One of the secrets of great leadership in any walk of life is to place those close to you who are not simply yes-men but who are prepared to be honest with you when they see you making a mistake. This is absolutely critical in the church: having true friends who speak the truth in love is vital.

I think of church leaders who simply became such objects of adulation by their people and by the wider evangelical world that, when they fell, it was clear that they had simply come to be regarded as too big to be held accountable. Nobody dared call them to account; nobody ever even suspected they needed to be held to account. I can think of others who simply started to believe their own propaganda and saw any and every criticism as a personal attack. Such people were disasters waiting to happen; and their problem was that they lost sight of the basics of the Christian life and made themselves accountable to no one. And I am always amazed at the cronies such people manage to gather around themselves: there is always someone willing to stroke the ego of such types, to tell them how wonderful they are whatever shenanigans they get up to; yet a true friend knows the necessity of speaking the truth out of love in all circumstances.

DOWNES: What signs of potential doctrinal drift and danger do you need to keep an eye out for in ministerial students?

TRUEMAN: I am increasingly convinced that pride is the root of problems among students. I was convicted recently by a minister friend quoting to me 1 Timothy 1:5-7 (ESV):

> The aim of our charge is love that issues from a pure heart and a good conscience and a sincere faith. Certain persons, by swerving from these, have wandered away into vain discussion, desiring to be teachers of the law, without understanding either what they are saying or the things about which they make confident assertions.

My friend made two observations about this passage. First, the drift into dubious theological discussion is here described as moral in origin: these characters have swerved from a pure heart, a good conscience, and a sincere faith; that is why their theology is so dreadful. Second, their desire is not to teach but *to be teachers*. There is an important difference here: their focus is on their own status, not on the words they proclaim. At most, the latter are merely instrumental to getting them status and boosting their careers.

Thus, what concerns me most is that students may simply *desire to be teachers*. If that is their motivation, then they have already abandoned a pure heart, a good conscience, and a sincere faith, and their theology, no matter how orthodox, is just a means to an end and no sound thing. It is why I am very sceptical of the internal call to the ministry as a decisive or motivating factor in seeking ordination. Nine times out of ten, I believe that the church should first discern who should be considering the Christian ministry, not simply a rubber-stamp act as a putative internal call which an individual may think he has.

Further, such students whose first desire is to be teachers are more likely to try to catch whatever is the latest trendy wave. Orthodoxy is always doomed to seem uncreative and pedestrian in the wider arena; if the aim is to be a teacher, to be the big shot, then it is more likely that orthodoxy will be less appealing in the long run – though there are those for whom orthodoxy too is simply a means to being a celebrity.

If a prideful desire to be a teacher, to be a somebody, is the fundamental problem, then one other aspect which is increasingly problematic is the whole phenomenon of the internet. Now anyone can put their views out for public consumption, without the usual processes of accountability, peer review, careful editing, timely reflection, etc., which is the norm in the scholarly world and has also been the tradition in the more theologically responsible parts of the Christian publishing industry. The internet has few quality controls and feeds narcissism. Again, I have a friend, a minister in a North American Presbyterian denomination who says that, as he reads many blogs, his overwhelming feeling is one of sadness as he sees men seriously undermining their future ministry through the venom they pour out on others. I think he is right.

Of course, all young theologians and aspiring church leaders say stupid and unpleasant things. I still blush about comments I made fifteen or twenty years ago which now seem arrogant and offensive, and certainly unworthy of a Christian. But for those of us who are older, the sins of our youth are thankfully now long vanished from the public sphere; yet such sins committed today can live on indefinitely in cyberspace. I shudder for those who have not yet grasped this basic fact and who say some frightful things on the internet which will come back to haunt them the very first time a church googles their name as part of doing routine background checks on a potential ministerial candidate. But more than that: I shudder at the kind of self-appointed arrogance among ministerial candidates and recently-minted graduates which the internet can foster and intensify.

Paul's words to Timothy seem prophetic in times such as ours. Students should cultivate pure hearts, good consciences, and a sincere faith. That way they will safeguard their theology from becoming idle speculation.

DOWNES: If theological poison flows from the professor, to the pastor, to the pew, how can this insidious effect be kept in check?

TRUEMAN: As for professors, no system is ideal because a system is only as good as the people who make it possible; but I do believe seminaries should be accountable to a church. Now, I am a professor at an independent seminary, and I regard neither my position nor the Seminary's constitution as sinful or wrong, simply as potentially more problematic.

As we serve the church, so I think it makes more sense for us to be directly linked to the church. That has not been without its historical problems: arguably the church link is what pulled Princeton down – one reason why J. Gresham Machen determined that Westminster should be independent; but on the whole it strikes me as better. Failing that link, I am increasingly persuaded that those who train men for the ministry should be officers of the church. That at least preserves ecclesiastical accountability through the status of individual professors.

As for pastors, I was once a Baptist but am now a convinced confessional Presbyterian, and the single most significant matter which made me make this shift was the issue of ministerial accountability to a clear and coherent confessional position, with an appropriate ecclesiastical structure to regulate this. The existence of presbyteries should, in theory at least, allow for the careful monitoring and evaluation of what is being taught from denominational pulpits. Of course, as noted above, the effectiveness of the system is only as good as the men who are part of it, but I do believe the presbyterian form of government comes closest to what is described in the New Testament and thus is the best system there is.

As for the people, I am impressed by the seventeenth-century practice of catechizing during house-to-house visitation as a means of reinforcing what is preached from the pulpit and monitoring the penetration of the preaching into the hearts and minds of individual believers. Now, I am not sure that going from door to door, hammering on about the Shorter Catechism is necessarily the right way to go (though there are many worse things that could be done); but it seems to me that, if this particular practice is now not appropriate, the need of the hour is to find the modern-day equivalent in order to make sure that the great gospel truths and duties contained in the Word of God are clearly grasped by every believer.

Downes: You once described the contribution of liberalism to the church as 'emptying pews and lives.' How did such a destructive movement succeed in capturing the churches?

Trueman: At a theoretical level, easy: the truth will always be opposed; falsehood will always prove more attractive in the long run to the unregenerate human heart. Of course, the path of liberalism was different in different nations and denominations since particular cultural, economic, social and political factors determined how the battle between truth and falsehood played out; but the basic moral dynamic is universal.

I do think that the culture of evangelicalism itself has often not helped. Belief in the truth is always difficult – doctrinally and morally. We believe not because we find it easy or straightforward but because we are commanded so to do. Yet evangelical culture often fails to acknowledge the level of struggle involved in being orthodox and thus creates unrealistic expectations for the Christian life.

Berkouwer says of Herman Bavinck (perhaps the outstanding Reformed theologian of the last two hundred years) that the people who most angered him were those who believed exactly what he did himself, but who failed to see the problems and difficulties, the sheer struggle, involved in so doing. I carried a copy of that anecdote in my wallet for many years as I worked in university departments where my faith was constantly under challenge from friends and colleagues as a reminder that the intellectual struggles I felt were precisely to be expected in the normal Christian life; but that I had to continue to believe not because it was easy or pain-free but because of God's revealed command so to do.

The pastoral significance of this is that too often we fail to present orthodoxy as such a struggle, giving people unrealistic expectations and the false alternatives of believing easily or believing nothing at all. That is a cruel dilemma to place before people, and one that must in practice ultimately favor the 'believe nothing' option for as soon as a struggle arises, the believer has nowhere to go.

DOWNES: In your estimation are there contemporary moods and movements that could have the same effect on the church as liberalism did?

TRUEMAN: Of course. For example, the pop-appropriation of some of the sillier excesses of postmodernism by numerous writers seems to be little more than the old liberalism *redivivus*: God is silenced, His demands on human beings are rendered equivocal, theology becomes the solipsistic musings of human beings, albeit refracted through communitarian views of language as opposed to the Kantian categories of the individual self-consciousness of the old-style liberalism.

I am also concerned at the loss of the sense of God's holiness in much that passes for theological reflection. Ideas of eternal significance are batted around like ping-pong balls. The awesome holiness of God should act as a control on speculation; yet there is little evidence of that in the contemporary scene. Again, the difficulty of belief is perhaps relevant here: if you find it easy to talk of God's holiness or

His wrath, then maybe you have never really wrestled with these doctrines. Barth's comment that all theology should be doxology is surely pertinent here.

DOWNES: The accusation has been made that evangelicals in the second half of the twentieth century went after recognition and prestige in the academy like Gadarene swine. As someone who previously taught at two British universities were you tempted to follow this trend? How did you resist?

TRUEMAN: No. Being sinlessly perfect I can honestly say I never felt that temptation but have always worked solely for the glory of God and the benefit of others. Come on, Martin, of course I did. All fallen human beings are narcissists at heart; we all want recognition, whether on the sporting field or in the workplace. I guess I am in the fortunate position, as a historian, of being able to have my cake and eat it: the scholarly guild within which I work has little interest in my theological commitments, and I can believe mad stuff like the Westminster Standards without my scholarly peers regarding that as anything other than an eccentric aberration.

Were I in systematic theology or ethics or one of the biblical fields, it would be much harder to be both a respected member of the academy and a confessional Christian. Of course, evangelicals working in those areas knew what they were getting into, so this should not surprise them; but I do think we need to pray for and support such colleagues who face unique and brutal challenges to their faith almost every day of their lives and who may well have to make a key choice between acceptance by the guild and fidelity to God's Word.

Having said that, I do think there is a distinction to be made between academic integrity and academic respect-ability. The failure to distinguish these two – and to fall into line with the scholarly guilds who determine the former on the basis of the latter – is problematic; and I do not think that evangelicals have thought critically enough about the very structure of scholarly guilds and discourse in a way that allows them to make this distinction in as useful and practical a way as they should. As soon as I hear the phrase 'but no biblical scholar believes that anymore' my antennae go up; that's not an argument, that's a rhetorical 'consent of the nations' ploy, whatever the merits of the particular case in point. The desire to be thought well of by all is seductive; and evangelical success in the academy needs to be assessed not in terms of who is invited to speak on which scholarly platform, but who has remained faithful to God's Word, despite all the pressure to do otherwise.

DOWNES: Why have evangelicals reduced the great Protestant confessions down to minimal statements?

TRUEMAN: Because evangelicalism, as a transdenominational, parachurch movement, needs to sideline great swathes of the faith in order to hold the alliance together. That is not a bad thing in itself. I identify myself as an evangelical and am very happy to be in common cause with brothers and sisters from other denominations who share basic commitments to the gospel. Such parachurch alliances are important in presenting a popular front for the gospel in the current climate.

Popular front evangelicalism only becomes a problem when, with its minimal doctrinal basis, it comes to be normative for how we actually understand Christianity and thus to impact how we understand the church. Then we find ourselves in a situation where tail wags dog, so to speak, where the identity of the church is shaped not by her own confession but by the exigencies of the evangelical world, where key theological issues such as divine sovereignty, baptism, and the Lord's Supper are marginalized. Wherever we come down on these issues, Scripture does teach about them; and we have no right to make them merely negotiable matters of indifference in the church. At the ecclesiastical level, I would rather do business with a convinced Arminian or Baptist who knows that the Bible's teaching on the pertinent issues are important, than with someone who thinks it is all a bit unclear and not that vital anyway.

The long-term impact of abandoning the historic confessions and catechisms is wide-ranging. You stand to lose much historical identity and sense of continuity with the past. With no catechisms and confessions of any depth, you have few resources left in the face of a rising tide of theological illiteracy which leaves the way open for all manner of weird and wonderful stuff to fill the resulting vacuum. You can end up simply replacing them with doctrinal statements which, through their very minimal nature are inherently unstable. And you might find you have a theology which is unsatisfying and ultimately of little use in providing a base from which to address many of the great issues of life.

None of this is to invest historic confessions and catechisms with the authority proper to Scripture alone; but it is to point to them as serious ecclesiastical and historical attempts to wrestle with the great themes of Scripture. If you wish to abandon them, you are free to do so; but unless you can find something which does the job equally well, in just as comprehensive and catholic a fashion, you might want to think twice before you throw them away.

DOWNES: One increasingly gets the impression that evangelicals are at a crossroads. There are plenty of voices urging them to go back to an 'ancient-future' faith, some are turning to Rome or Constantinople. Why should they go to Geneva instead?

TRUEMAN: Because Geneva, or Reformed Orthodoxy, as the project was originally conceived, offers precisely an ancient-future faith. The great works of Reformed Orthodoxy and the impressive catechisms and confessions of the sixteenth century are all built upon positive reception of the ancient creeds and even the best of medieval theology.

If I have made any contribution to the understanding of Reformed Orthodoxy, it is this: the Reformed faith at its best is a brilliant and catholic articulation of the Christian faith, as developed in the ancient church and Middle Ages, and then refracted though the necessary corrections made by Protestant exegetes and theologians in the sixteenth and seventeenth centuries. Only as the notion of 'Scripture alone' has been wrested from context and come to be understood as 'we only need to read the Bible' has this catholic and historic dimension been lost. This has then been compounded by the abandonment of the great creeds, confessions and catechisms in our church practice. Reformed Orthodoxy gives you the best of the Christian creedal tradition, combined with vital Protestant insights such as justification by grace through faith, and the centrality of assurance to Christian experience.

The loss of historical rootedness and identity which evangelicalism seems to have experienced has left us vulnerable to the attractions of Rome and Constantinople; but it does not have to be that way. Evangelicalism has sold its birthright; we should reclaim it before it is too late.

Downes: Tertullian regarded Pagan philosophy as the parent and instigator of heresy. A good case could be made that many heresies are in substance based on human philosophy but are dressed up in Christian language. Is this true? Do we see contemporary examples of this?

Trueman: To an extent, though I am always a little concerned that such sound-bites as those of Tertullian can take on a life of their own. All theology is to some extent parasitic upon the philosophical vocabulary of the traditionary context within which it is articulated; and the mere presence of, say, Greek philosophical terms and logic in a theological statement do not indicate that the statement is necessarily an unholy synthesis of Jerusalem and Athens.

I am more attracted to Cardinal Newman's statement that every heresy was actually a Christian truth pushed too far and to the exclusion of other truths. Thus, Arianism was in origin an attempt to defend the transcendence of God the Father in a way that ultimately prevented a biblical understanding of the Son. Modalism emphasized divine unity at the expense of divine threeness. Ebionitism emphasized Christ's humanity in a way that precluded a biblical account of His divinity. Etc. etc. The key is always biblical balance, allowing God's revelation to check our speculations.

As to contemporary examples: open theism is an attempt to underscore human moral responsibility and to distance God from sin; but this is done at the expense of God's sovereignty; prosperity teaching is an attempt to emphasize the importance of praying to a God who wants the best for His people, but in a way that conflates human aspirations with God's purposes. These are just two examples; there are plenty of others.

DOWNES: When a denomination or Christian organization falls into serious theological error does history give us any encouragement that the situation can be retrieved?

TRUEMAN: Not much. There is the remarkable turnaround in the Southern Baptist Convention over recent decades, symbolized more than anything else by the conservative takeover of the Southern Baptist Seminary in Louisville under the presidency of Dr Albert Mohler. That is impressive but I would guess there are structures in place within the organization that helped facilitate the move.

Beyond that, however, the picture is not so good. The Anglican evangelical approach of operating at a local level has certainly had an impact in individual parishes, and has led to some great church-planting developments, but has failed to shift the larger denomination in a more faithful direction, at least in Britain. When it is big news that a bishop defends the resurrection, we should rightly rejoice; but we should also realize that the overall doctrinal bar must be set pretty low when adherence to such a basic doctrine by a church leader is newsworthy. The Church of Scotland is no better. Encouragements at local level, but no real headway in the presbyteries or in ministerial training, where gains are only ever made in one area by selling out in others. You cannot reform the church without taking heat; that is what men like Dr Mohler had to do; and that is what the evangelicals in mixed denominations need to do at an institutional level.

But God is sovereign. He will build His kingdom through the power of His gospel, despite the weaknesses and failings of His church.

CHAPTER THREE

IN MY PLACE CONDEMNED HE STOOD

An Interview on Penal Substitution with Tom Schreiner

Dr Tom Schreiner is the Associate Dean and Professor of New Testament at Southern Baptist Theological Seminary, Louisville, Kentucky. He is the author of numerous books including *New Testament Theology: Magnifying God in Christ* and a contributor to *The Nature of the Atonement: Four Views*.

MARTIN DOWNES: As a teacher of New Testament interpretation are you surprised by the effort to debunk penal substitution on exegetical grounds?

TOM SCHREINER: Nothing surprises me, for alternate interpretations are proposed of every major doctrine, including the deity of Christ and the Trinity.

DOWNES: Are errors connected with penal substitution best combatted by giving better attention to theological method as well as on exegetical grounds?

SCHREINER: The primary issue is always exegesis, but theological method is important as well.

43

DOWNES: How significant is the denial of penal substitution?

SCHREINER: I think it is very significant, for penal substitution is the heart of the atonement and the basis of forgiveness of sins.

DOWNES: Should we speak of 'God punishing Jesus' on the cross?

SCHREINER: It depends upon what we mean. If we mean that God is angry and forces His Son to bear His wrath, the answer is clearly no. But the Biblical view is that a loving Father sent the Son (who voluntarily gave His life) to satisfy His wrath. Hence, the Father did punish the Son, but He did so because of His great love for sinners.

DOWNES: What would be your pastoral approach to a minister in training who denied penal substitution and a professor at an evangelical college or seminary who held the same views?

SCHREINER: I would be patient with a student and try to persuade them of the biblical standpoint. Patience is initially the right stance for a professor as well. But if a professor comes to a settled conviction against penal substitution, he should be removed from his position in my judgment.

DOWNES: How important is the doctrine of penal substitution to evangelical unity?

SCHREINER: It is crucial, for all unity must be based on the truth of the gospel, and without penal substitution there is no gospel.

DOWNES: How would you help someone to understand that penal substitution is central to understanding the atonement?

SCHREINER: I would take them step by step through the scriptures showing 1) God's matchless holiness; 2) the sin of human beings; 3) the eternal judgment that is deserved; and 4) the sin-bearing death and resurrection of Jesus Christ for sinners.

DOWNES: Defenders of penal substitution today are sometimes accused of holding to a more extreme version of the doctrine which those who appear to be denying that doctrine are reacting against. Do you think this is true?

SCHREINER: I don't think it is true at all. Some popular illustrations distort the doctrine, but evangelical scholarship has presented penal substitution fairly for years.

DOWNES: What books on the atonement are a 'must read' for pastors?

SCHREINER: *The Cross of Christ* by John Stott, *The Apostolic Preaching of the Cross* by Leon Morris, *Pierced For Our Transgressions by* Ovey, Sach and Jeffrey, and *Where Wrath and Mercy Meet* edited by David Peterson.

DOWNES: How do you account for the recent resurgence of opposition to penal substitution within (of all places) mainstream Western evangelicalism?

SCHREINER: The cross is always an offense, and today any notion of punishment is alien to our world-view where love 'swallows up' for many the biblical teaching on God's holiness.

DOWNES: Why do you think we are seeing self-identifying evangelicals using similar arguments against penal substitution that were once employed by Socinians and liberals?

SCHREINER: Many of them are ignorant of history, and some of them unfortunately are inclining in a more liberal direction.

DOWNES: As you think of present denials and positive affirmations of penal substitution, what are your hopes and fears for this doctrine as it is taught and believed in evangelicalism?

SCHREINER: I hope that recent robust defenses of penal substitution will help us to see afresh that penal substitution is the heart of the gospel. Every generation must relearn and re-teach the gospel afresh. The fear is that heresy might spread among our generation.

Chapter Four

THE AGONY OF DECEIT

An Interview
with Michael Horton

Michael Scott Horton teaches Apologetics and Systematic Theology at Westminster Seminary California, Escondido, California. He is editor-in-chief of *Modern Reformation* magazine, and hosts the White Horse Inn radio broadcast. He is the author of numerous books including, *God of Promise: Introducing Covenant Theology*, and *Putting Amazing Back Into Grace*.

MARTIN DOWNES: As you reflect back to your days in seminary and early years in the ministry were there men who started out with evangelical convictions who later moved away from the gospel? How did you cope with that?

MICHAEL HORTON: I cannot think of anyone with whom I attended seminary who has drifted from evangelical convictions. If there are such cases, I'm just not aware of them. Beyond my seminary circle, I have seen friends – pastors, ordinands, and laypeople – leave evangelical and Reformed churches for Roman Catholic and Eastern Orthodox bodies. A few have joined mainline Protestant churches that I knew were Liberal, but the social and political agenda trumped theology.

In each of these cases, depending in part on the relationship, I responded differently. At least in the US, there has been a trend among those raised in conservative evangelical churches to move toward more liturgical churches. A lot of younger evangelicals were reared in 'happy-clappy' churches with theater seating, a praise band, singing off the wall (both literally and figuratively). They are looking for reverence, history, mystery and transcendence. A lot of them are looking for doctrine, too, oddly enough. According to one *Wall Street Journal* study, in fact, the number one element that young urban professionals in New York said they would look for if they decided to go back to church: theological discussion groups! I guess I'm getting older.

To me, the megachurch movement was contemporary, but now it's old news and the generation that was raised in it is now looking for something more serious, meaningful, beautiful, and truthful. Of course, 'mystery' and 'transcendence' can be a dangerous drug as well, if the object is something other than the Triune God and His revelation in Jesus Christ.

I hope I'm not being too simplistic when I say that in each of these cases in which exits were made to Rome, Orthodoxy or Liberalism, it has been due significantly to the fact that the justification of the ungodly by grace alone through faith alone has not been truly understood, affirmed, or at least been made a central concern.

Downes: Have you ever been drawn toward any views or movements that time has shown to have been unhelpful or even dangerous theologically?

Horton: Many of us are reacting against something. In planning a dinner party, we all know not to invite our friends recently converted out of Roman Catholicism, at least if we are looking to host a pleasant and light-hearted evening. The same is true of evangelicals who have just discovered the 'five points of Calvinism' (we call it the 'cage phase').

Ex-fundamentalists may be drawn to certain aspects of liberalism that ex-liberals find completely abhorrent. In sharp contrast to the fairly recent past, churches today are rarely composed of people from a relatively similar background. But somehow, despite such diverse experiences, we form a body and it may be that the immigrants to the gospel from one extreme help to keep those from another extreme from keeping the pendulum swinging.

Fundamentalism – or at least a very conservative evangelicalism – was my background, so my tendency has been to react viscerally against certain aspects of this movement, while being too willing at times to give non-evangelicals the benefit of the doubt. Of course, that is not fair or loving to my neighbor, who may still have something important to teach me.

I've never really been drawn to Liberalism, Roman Catholicism, Eastern Orthodoxy. There's just not enough of the gospel there. However, I can sympathize with those evangelicals who have, since I've experienced the same knee-jerk reactions. A lot of 'new liberals' are former fundamentalists and evangelicals who have retained a reactionary and narrow-minded attitude.

Downes: How should a minister keep his heart, mind and will from theological error?

Horton: Special investigators of counterfeiting schemes study real treasury notes and coins with meticulous care before they learn anything else. Then they can spot the fraud a mile away. I am often astonished at the degree to which laypeople often know what they believe and why they believe it more than their pastors. How is it that people who are called to various secular vocations find the time for this while many pastors (despite the job description found in the New Testament) apparently do not? Ministers are often expected to be CEOs, managers, therapists and coaches – just about anything other than shepherds who answer our Lord's mandate to Peter: 'Feed my sheep.'

I think that we have to resist every attempt to turn our *studies* into *offices*. An open-door policy is not necessarily virtuous. It is often more helpful to the body if the minister closes the door, with an eagerness to mine the treasures of God's Word. The diaconate was established in the first place so that the apostles and pastors could devote themselves to the Word and to prayer.

I believe that one of the primary responsibilities of the elders is to ensure that the minister is free to meditate prayerfully on God's Word, read great books and take part in conferences or other forms of continuing education – and to ensure that this is in fact happening.

There is certainly a place for responding directly to specific theological errors, but a ministry devoted to feeding the sheep (beginning with the minister and elders) will yield a mature flock that is less likely to be distracted from the truth as it is in Christ.

Downes: You have been involved in writing and editing several books dealing with contemporary theological errors. Have these books merely strengthened those already in agreement with you theologically or have they also helped the confused, and convinced those in error?

Horton: There is certainly a place for both strengthening the persuaded as well as persuading others. The pull of the tide toward human-centered religion is powerful and it is not uncommon to see otherwise discerning people swept out to sea.

At the same time, I've been greatly encouraged by the responses I've received from pastors, church officers and laypeople who tell me that God used one of my books to help bring them to a better understanding of the gospel. In between my failings and half-hearted attempts, there has been nothing more encouraging than that report.

Downes: Hilary of Poitiers said that 'Heresy lies in the sense assigned, not in the word written. The guilt is that of the expositor, not of the text.' What are the danger signs of this very thing happening in a man's ministry?

HORTON: Calvin (who was an appreciative reader of Hilary) also said something similar with respect to the way the East and the West developed different ways of speaking about the Trinity. A fellow Christian may be saying exactly the same thing while using concepts, analogies and terms that are less familiar to us, while someone else uses the right words but doesn't actually intend them the same way.

Liberals, of course, are notorious examples of this latter tendency. They still use the orthodox vocabulary, but mean something completely different by it.

I always enjoy conversations with my Lutheran friends. At first, the difference in our paradigms makes us think that our disagreements are greater than they are, but when we patiently attend to what the other is *saying*, we often realize that on some points at least we really are not that far apart. Yet our traditions have typically said, 'If you don't say things the way we do, you're not really affirming what we affirm.' So if Lutherans don't like our 'TULIP', they must be Arminians, when in fact they are strict monergists (salvation by God's work alone) and sharply reject Arminianism. We still disagree on important issues, but on others it's more a matter of different paradigms, categories and vocabulary. We should never raise those to the normative level of Scripture.

DOWNES: Are heresies best combated by giving better attention to theological method rather than just matters of exegesis?

HORTON: I think there are two dangers here. One is to build a sophisticated theory of truth (epistemology) on some supposedly neutral and universal foundation – and then erect our Christian doctrine on top of it. At the other extreme are those who think that we can ignore epistemology and apologetics and just get on with the business of telling and living the Christian story.

In my book, *Covenant and Eschatology*, I tried to walk that tightrope. If God is the author of all reality, then He is also the source of our access to it. However, Scripture does not explain everything that exists or how we can know it. Here we are dependent, like anyone else, on God's common grace. With the wisdom that comes from the truth revealed in Scripture, we study a variety of thinkers in many disciplines. Because of total depravity, unbelievers suppress and distort the truth, but they cannot suppress everything at the same time.

Cornelius Van Til used the analogy of a beach ball that keeps popping up when children try to push it down under the water.

I've learned a lot from non-Christians about fixing my car, managing my finances, and even practical suggestions for child-rearing. But I've also learned a lot from non-Christians about history, philosophy, art, science and culture. None of us can claim independence from the dominant thought-forms of our age, so the best procedure is to expose our presuppositions and bring them to Christ for judgment according to His Word.

We're naïve if we think that exegesis is blissfully preserved from the biases that we carry around with us as citizens of our time and place. And we are naïve if we think that exegesis is independent of our theological convictions that we have as a result of our covenantal nurture in particular traditions.

No one reads the Bible alone (although the essence of heresy – *haeresis* – means 'going one's own way'), so the goal should be to read the Bible together with the wider church and to form our convictions together, as long as the church to which we belong places itself *under* God's Word.

Sola scriptura has never meant, at least for the churches of the Reformation, that the Bible tells us *everything*, but that it (a) teaches us everything we need to know for doctrine and life and (b) is the only *normative* authority for our faith and practice.

I'm always amazed at the great variety in philosophical assumptions and vocabularies among the great teachers of the church through the ages. Like the East, the Western church has been heavily influenced by Platonism and Neoplatonism. When I disagree with Augustine, for example, it's usually because I think he's too indebted to this philosophical inheritance. Yet I find more agreement with him *in doctrine* than I do with many whose philosophical leanings might be more similar to my own.

Even at the Westminster Assembly, there were divines who were more inclined to Plato, others to Aristotle, still others to anti-Aristotelian Ramist thought; some Thomists, some Scotists, and so forth. But none of these differences erupted into debate as they agreed on a common confession. Christian doctrine can be warped by our secular constructs, but it has an uncanny way of warping the secular constructs themselves and pressing them into service to Christ.

DOWNES: How have you dealt with church members or students who have been attracted to, or taken in by false teaching?

HORTON: Pastoral sensitivity and prudence is required in order to know whether a fellow-Christian needs 'Law' or 'Gospel'. (A terrific discussion of this is found in William Perkins' *The Art of Prophesying*.) So an obstinate person who persists in heresy should be warned with the threat of excommunication (as Paul treated the Galatians).

However, a struggling Christian who has been exposed to false teaching must be corrected with patience and love. This person is a bruised reed or a flickering candle, and we know how Christ treats them – for to some degree, we are all in this category.

Even excommunication has as its goal the evangelical repentance of the heretic as well as the peace and purity of the rest of the flock; therefore, even the obstinate should be threatened with the law, with the clear proclamation of the gospel constantly held out to them.

Christ displays His wisdom and care for us by instituting a church that bears His appointed marks: the Word rightly preached, the sacraments rightly administered, and discipline rightly exercised. In this way, it is Christ Himself – through His ordained ministry – and not through vigilantes and heresy hunters who guards His own.

Following the examples of Matthew 18 and Acts 15, we bring the matter to the individual, then to the local church leadership, and then – if the offender will still not heed the church's rebuke – the case is brought before the wider church in its broader assemblies.

DOWNES: How should a pastor protect the flock and help them to value sound doctrine when he knows that they could well be influenced by an overload of unhelpful teaching from books, conferences, television, and the internet?

HORTON: My response to this question flows out of the previous one. We not only need to teach people the truth about God, humanity, Christ's person and work, and the way of salvation and godliness; we need to teach them about the church. The doctrine of the church (ecclesiology) is relatively thin in evangelical circles today, despite the place that it has had historically in Reformed faith and practice.

When we read (as in Ephesians 4) that Christ, in His ascension, has poured out on His church the gift of pastors and teachers, the reference is not to the invisible church but to the visible church. For many evangelicals, the invisible church is all there is. 'The church' is simply all those who are born again. Without denying that important truth, we need to recognize that the visible church is that body that consists of all professing believers together with their children. How many times do we read in the epistles of the need to submit to the leaders of the church who watch over us for our good?

I've given considerable time to combatting TV preachers and popular writers who have grossly distorted the gospel. An important motive for this is that many members of our own churches are drawn to these voices. However, churches that emphasize the priority of submitting to the teaching of those whom God has *sent* (i.e., commissioned and ordained by the laying on of hands), who themselves are accountable to the creeds and confessions as well as to the discipline of broader assemblies, will help their members to drink from the wells that give them life.

Again, lighting candles will be more effective in the long run than cursing the darkness. Are our churches well taught? Are our sermons drawn from deep wells, holding Christ forth as the prophet, priest and king? Are we catechizing our young people? Is the Word communicated not only in the sermon and in teaching but also in the liturgy? Is the goal of our singing 'so that the Word of Christ may dwell in us richly' (Col. 3:16)? Do we regularly celebrate the Lord's Supper and regard it as indispensable for the health of our flock? Are our elders regularly visiting members, helping families to flourish in the covenant of grace?

Churches that are doing their job of saturating their people with gospel-centered preaching, teaching, worship, sacraments, prayer, fellowship and discipline, will yield a maturity that will be more resistant to being blown back and forth with every wind of doctrine. That is exactly the argument that Paul makes in Ephesians 4.

DOWNES: Reformed or conservative Christians are sometimes accused of having an unhealthy interest in controversy and polemics. Is this a fair comment?

HORTON: In my view, the short answer, unfortunately, is 'yes'. We are often known more for what we're against than by what we're for.

In Acts 2, the church was identified by its devotion to the apostles' teaching, the breaking of the bread, the fellowship, the prayers, and an intense evangelistic and missionary zeal. We read repeatedly throughout Acts not only that the Word of God was faithfully *taught*, but that it *spread*. Today, we are often pressed to choose between getting the gospel *right* and getting the gospel *out*. If the gospel is the good news that we say that it is – sinners reconciled to a holy God through the work of Christ alone – why shouldn't we be the vanguard of outreach to the world?

I fear that it all comes down to sloth or laziness, and I include myself in that critique. Conservatives are often enthusiastic about the truth, but lazy about mission; progressives are often enthusiastic about mission and lazy about the truth.

Rick Warren, the popular California pastor, has reissued the familiar call for 'deeds, not creeds'. But this is to say 'law, not gospel'; command without promise; imperatives without indicatives. We need to put these together again. There is the triumphant announcement, 'All authority in heaven and on earth has been given to me', 'here is what you are in Christ', followed by the 'Therefore, go', 'do/do not', etc. If we don't get the message right, the mission is just some version of works-righteousness; if we don't get the mission right, then we are thinking only of ourselves. The mission flows out of the message.

DOWNES: It is natural that a younger generation can find it harder to navigate the theological currents in the church. What advice would you give to younger ministers as they assess and handle various movements today?

HORTON: Of course, it has always been difficult for ministers to navigate in this passing evil age, but the good news is that Christ, by His Word and Spirit, has always been keeping His promise not only to preserve the church but beat down the gates of hell. Christ has already triumphed over Satan, death and hell! That is the good news without which I could not muster the confidence to enter the pulpit or the classroom.

Whether young or old, ministers should, in my view, keep themselves acquainted with both the wisdom of the past and the currents of the day. Paul's instruction to Timothy is not only to preach the truth but to combat falsehood. Falsehood always has an element of truth.

Those who are attracted to spiritual fads and fashions often find a few good reasons for it. We have to appreciate the draw of these intellectual and popular movements. Again, this takes a lot of time and energy in study. However, it is indispensable for our ministry.

DOWNES: What is the best way for a busy pastor to keep himself informed of contemporary theological issues when he knows that there is simply not enough time to read all the books. Could you name some of these critical issues and the best material on them?

HORTON: I'll restrict myself to issues of greatest relevance to evangelical and Reformed churches. The Emerging Church movement is one example. Reacting against both fundamentalism and the megachurch movement, many younger Christians are looking for a richer and more varied experience, a mosaic that reflects not only our increasingly diverse cultures but denominations and traditions.

In practice, this often means smaller gatherings in which worshipers move from station-to-station: an area with candles and icons, another with a prayer labyrinth, another for sitting on pillows or couches to hear someone lead a discussion. There is considerable variety in theological orientation among these groups, but it is common to hear readings not only from ancient and medieval Christian writers but from Thomas Merton, Buddhists, and a variety of poets or novelists. The ambiance is definitely 'mystical', in sharp contrast to the theatrics of their megachurch youth.

Brian McLaren is the best-known leader in this movement. In my estimation (confirmed by some leaders within the movement itself), McLaren's eclecticism and openness are mostly directed toward mysticism (Christian and Buddhist), Anabaptism, 'high-church' traditions and Liberalism. He is sharply critical of conservative evangelicalism and especially of confessional Reformed theology.

Following McLaren, many in this circle claim that their movement is 'postmodern', although this claim seems to me as dubious as the term 'postmodern' is ambiguous. I have participated in discussions with McLaren and others in this group, with results published as *The Church in Emerging Culture,* ed. Leonard Sweet (Zondervan, 2003). There is also D. A. Carson's *Becoming Conversant with the Emergent Church,* (Zondervan, 2005).

The series of works by David Wells, beginning with *No Place for Truth,* (Eerdmans, 1993), illuminates the challenges of our time more broadly. I have written or edited a number of books along similar lines, but it would be out of place, especially for a British audience, to push my own books! Nevertheless, I might mention the series I have been writing that tries to bring classic Reformed theology into conversation with contemporary issues and resources.

The first volume, *Covenant and Eschatology,* is a prolegomenon of sorts; *Lord and Servant* treats the doctrine of God, humanity and christology (including the atonement in the light of contemporary criticisms); *Covenant and Salvation* treats justification and union with Christ in conversation with the New Perspective on Paul and Radical Orthodoxy.

I'm finishing up the last volume, *People and Place,* exploring ecclesiology. The series is published by Westminster John Knox (WJK). I might also mention James K. A. Smith's *Who's Afraid of Postmodernism?* (Baker Academic, 2006). Sometimes there is an over-reaction to 'postmodernism' in our circles, as if modernity did us any favors! While one might not agree with everything, Smith is alert to some of the dangers of postmodern thinking while pointing up its insights.

DOWNES: How can a minister keep himself from bitterness, pride and cynicism as he faces controversy?

HORTON: Only the Spirit of Christ can produce within us the fruit of the Spirit. I wish I could say that I yielded to the Spirit's guidance in eliminating the fruit of the flesh, but I am in need of daily forgiveness and repentance on these as on other points.

However, it helps put things in perspective when I recall that the same grace that opened my eyes to the gospel keeps me growing in that faith and preserves me from many of the errors to which I am prone.

With Isaiah, I can only say, 'I am undone, for I am a man of unclean lips and dwell among a people of unclean lips.' When I am bitter, proud or cynical, I am assuming the stance of the Pharisee in Jesus' parable – even as I set myself up as a defender of the publican. What do we have that we have not been given?

The gospel is sufficient not only for our justification but for our sanctification as well. As we are saved by grace, we grow by grace and this leaves no room for pride.

Besides being sin, pride is a waste of time. I still have plenty of error to unlearn and truth to learn. The Christian life is a pilgrimage, not a pedestal.

DOWNES: Knowing that pastoral ministry involves proclaiming peace and waging war against the strongholds of false doctrine in the church, who in your estimation has set a good model for younger ministers to emulate in these areas?

HORTON: In addition to numerous colleagues, God has richly blessed me with friends and mentors like James Boice, R. C. Sproul, Robert Godfrey, David Wells and J. I. Packer.

From church history, I think especially of Irenaeus, Athanasius, Gregory of Nyssa, Ambrose, Augustine, Anselm; of course, Luther and Calvin are my main heroes, but I think also of Bucer, Knox and Cranmer as well as the Puritans (especially Perkins, Sibbes and Owen).

More recently, there has been the witness of people like Orr, Hodge, Warfield, Spurgeon, Lloyd-Jones and Stott. However, it's increasingly difficult to point to a particular tradition (as implied above) today as producing the main lot of exemplary pastors and theologians.

Ironically, some friends like Tom Oden and William Willimon (mainline Methodists) defend the doctrine of justification with more rigor and penetrating insight against contemporary detractors than some Reformed people.

In an age of confessional confusion, labels do not seem quite as relevant as they once were.

CHAPTER FIVE

THE FAITHFUL PASTOR

AND

THE FAITHFUL CHURCH

*An Interview
with Mark Dever*

Mark Dever is Senior Pastor of Capitol Hill Baptist Church in Washington, D. C. and serves as the Executive Director for 9 Marks ministeries. He is the author of *Nine Marks of a Healthy Church* and *The Deliberate Church*.

MARTIN DOWNES: As you reflect back to your days in seminary and early years in the ministry were there men who started out with evangelical convictions who later moved away from the gospel? How did you cope with that?

MARK DEVER: Not really. I myself had been an agnostic and became an evangelical Christian. So, I was part of the stream flowing in the opposite direction. When I read liberal books or had liberal professors in seminary, I was aware that many of them would have had their beginnings in evangelical Christianity, but I wasn't aware of their particular stories.

DOWNES: Have you ever been drawn toward any views or movements that time has shown to have been unhelpful or even dangerous theologically?

DEVER: Yes. I was involved in the Charismatic movement for a couple of years when I first became a Christian. The part of the Charismatic movement that I was involved in was mishandling Scripture. It tended to be too human – centered concentrating on how much 'faith' we had, and effectively de-emphasized the gospel that saves.

DOWNES: How should a minister keep his heart, mind and will from theological error?

DEVER: I would encourage a man to marry a woman who loves the Lord as much or more than he does, and to stay in the Word. I would also encourage him to build relationships with people in a sound Bible-preaching church.

DOWNES: Hilary of Poitiers said that 'Heresy lies in the sense assigned, not in the word written. The guilt is that of the expositor, not of the text.' What are the danger signs of this very thing happening in a man's ministry?

DEVER: The danger signs that I can think of would be avoiding honest relationships and playing fast and loose with the biblical text.

DOWNES: How have you dealt with church members or students who have been attracted or taken in by false teaching?

DEVER: My fundamental way of dealing with church members who seem to be attracted to false teaching is to provide good teaching regularly. If in God's providence that fails to be sufficient to keep them orthodox, then apart from some personal conversations or correspondence, I simply entrust them to the hands of God and concentrate on shepherding those sheep whom He has given me.

DOWNES: Why do men possessed of fine intellectual gifts end up embracing and believing significant theological errors?

DEVER: Go read 1 Corinthians 1. No one is saved by their intellect. God has determined to show His wisdom in ways that appear foolish to the wise of this world.

DOWNES: How can a minister discern the difference between those who are thinking their way through doctrines on the way to greater depth and clarity, and those who are questioning doctrines in a way that could lead to significant error?

DEVER: Being able to do this is basic to serving as a pastor. Is there a full cooperation in the life of the church with the person? Is there some immorality that it seems they are trying to justify? Do they seem to desire to follow God as much as they can see in Scripture?

DOWNES: How should a pastor protect the flock and help them to value sound doctrine when he knows that they could well be influenced by an overload of unhelpful teaching from books, conferences, television, and the internet?

DEVER: A pastor should give himself to faithful preaching and real relationships.

DOWNES: What would you consider to be the main theological dangers confronting us today and how can we deal with them?

DEVER: The main theological dangers I see confronting us today are a practical rejection of the authority of God's Word even by those who theoretically submit to it; a rejection of the sovereignty of God in favor of the putative sovereignty of man; a caricature, misunderstanding or rejection of the penal substitution of Christ for sinners; a shallow understanding of conversion as a mere shift of opinions; a worldliness in our evangelism which deceives people about the very nature of the gospel we are hoping to win them to; an individualism that de-centers the congregation from the life of a Christian; and a carelessness of churches in addressing members in unrepentant sin, which causes untold confusion about what it means to be a Christian. I think that we deal with these dangers by understanding and teaching what God has called the local church to be and, by His Spirit's power, working to be that.

DOWNES: It is natural that a younger generation can find it harder to navigate the theological currents in the church. What advice would you give to younger ministers as they assess and handle various movements today?

DEVER: I would encourage them to find reliable mentors and to trust them. Know the Word well yourself. Give yourself to the study of God's Word. Try to learn your own heart's deceptiveness and get others to try to help you recognize it. Read the best of authors, not the most popular. Be especially careful to investigate honestly doctrines that you think you don't like.

DOWNES: What is the best way for a busy pastor to keep informed of contemporary theological issues when he knows that there is simply not enough time to read all the books? Could you name a handful of critical issues and the best material on them.

DEVER: I don't know how important I think this is; I think that it is far more important to know the truth than to learn all of the counterfeits. Al Mohler, Don Carson, John Piper, David Wells, Ligon Duncan are a great early warning system.

Chapter Six

TRUTH, ERROR
AND
THE MINISTER'S TASK

*An Interview
with Derek Thomas*

Derek Thomas is Professor of Practical and Systematic Theology at Reformed Theological Seminary, and Minister of Teaching at First Presbyterian Church, Jackson, Mississippi. He is the editor of *Reformation 21* and has written numerous books including *Calvin's Teaching on Job* and *Let's Study Revelation*.

MARTIN DOWNES: As you reflect back to your days in seminary and early years in the ministry were there men who started out with evangelical convictions who later moved away from the gospel? How did you cope with that?

DEREK THOMAS: I cannot even think about this without first saying, 'there go I but for the grace of God'. Some, to be sure, were always more interested in the peripheral and speculative aspects of Christianity to stay the course.

But one individual that I think about almost every day for the past thirty years and more, a close friend at undergraduate university, was (and remains in my estimation) the most zealous 'Christian' I have known. This individual suddenly and decisively abandoned any profession of faith the week before graduation. The shock of it remains appallingly vivid to this day. I say 'Christian' because that is what it was, phenomenologically. To all outward appearances the marks of grace were there in abundance. Was this an example of Hebrews 6:4-6? Perhaps. I do not know. Eternity will tell. But it has kept me from presumption more than once, examining oneself lest there be in me an evil heart of unbelief.

DOWNES: Have you ever been drawn toward any views or movements that time has shown to have been unhelpful or even dangerous theologically?

THOMAS: Unless you consider my 'conversion' to paedo-baptism such (!), then No! Arrogant as that sounds. I have always been from the time of my conversion to this day (thirty-six years) a vanilla Calvinist of the experiential variety. I have developed a greater love for Calvin and though I do not accept the Calvin versus Calvinism school of thought, I have appreciated more and more the roots of seventeenth-century Puritanism.

DOWNES: How should a minister keep his heart, mind and will from theological error?

THOMAS: We are all capable of goofy ideas and sloppy exegetical insights. I try to make it a rule (and often tell my students) that I don't teach or preach ideas that have no basis in creedal/confessional formulation and have not passed the test of time.

I only whisper my 'insights' to my dog (who has a way of raising his ears suggesting that I'm way 'off base'). I have belonged to two denominations that require a clear assent to the Westminster Confession of Faith as well as a seminary that requires an annual re-affirmation of my assent. That helps me keep within the tracks of orthodoxy.

Of equal importance are things like: maintaining a close and daily watch on *my own* heart (1 Tim. 4:16); don't allow my calling to become a mere profession (to cite John Piper, *Brothers, We Are Not Professionals*); read and read and read oneself into a warm relationship with Christ by a balanced mixture of biographical and theological literature (I have found few 'devotional' books of any help, to be honest); keep the hymnbook close by; read and engage in an exercise of self-examination, something on justification on a regular basis (Lloyd-Jones on Romans 3:21 – 4:25 has been my regular way of doing it); maintain a love affair with Bunyan's *Pilgrim's Progress*; a pastor to the pastor and the importance of friends with whom we can be straightforwardly 'in your face'.

DOWNES: Calvin said that ministers have two voices. One is for the sheep and the other for warding off the wolves. How have you struck the right balance in this regard in your pulpit ministry?

THOMAS: Who could ever affirm that they have been 'balanced' here? It has been said of John Milton that he was better at portraying Paradise Lost than Paradise Regained, of hell rather than heaven, of condemnation rather than grace.

Ministers can so easily develop grudges and become angry and allow that anger to show itself in the pulpit justified as 'righteous anger', of course. The cause may be legion: pent-up frustration over poor remuneration, a bad marriage, a secret life of unmortified sin and pulpit anger is a smokescreen of anger at oneself, the Elijah syndrome ('I only am left') that ends up (unlike Elijah!) justifying majoring on minors (tertiary issues, if truth be told). I think this is the peculiar temptation of those who maintain an unapologetic Calvinistic theology.

DOWNES: Good men can end up with an excessively negative ministry when they become preoccupied with error. This of course was a point made by Dr Martyn Lloyd-Jones in his conversation with T. T. Shields. How can a minister keep himself from this temptation?

THOMAS: It is tempting in a culture where Bible-grounded proclamation is vilified and postmodern deconstruction contributes to a society where truth is relative and context-ualized to yield to the pressure leveled against being con-sidered 'negative'.

On that score, we must recall how often the moral code (Ten Commandments) is put in the negative. The over-reaction to excessive preoccupation with the negative can sometimes result in a Calvinism that is sickly and insipid. 'Winsome' is the word used in my circles, often suggesting an unwillingness to be overly assertive on issues that divide even when those issues are clearly taught in Scripture.

Still, the question is well put and it is often much easier to condemn than affirm and encourage. I have noticed, for example, that ministers are often the slowest to express thanks for other ministers' preaching. The development of Barnabas-like encouragement is a much needed gift within any church and it should begin with those of us who are preachers.

DOWNES: How do you cope with men who are sound in many ways, and whose ministries have been beneficial, but who, nonetheless, have held harmful views?

THOMAS: It is crucial to make the distinction that Paul makes between those things which are of 'first importance' and those things which are secondary (1 Cor. 15:3). It would be churlish not to profit from the towering genius of Richard Baxter, for example, despite his quasi-*Amyraldianism* or *neonomianism* (the subtlety of which is worthy of Aquinas). *The Reformed Pastor* is a classic worthy of being considered among the very best things written on pastoral ministry. I thank God for him and men like him with whom I disagree (sometimes strongly) on some things of huge importance.

I read and profit from a host of preachers (most of whom are dead) with whom I have many disagreements. I exercise (I pray) loving discernment and receive with thanks the good and equally reject what is bad. I am not, of course, bound to sit under their ministry every week or belong to their churches where practices may take place which violates conscience.

Here in the United States, for example, C. S. Lewis is raised to iconic status among conservative Christians, but if truth be told, his view of Scripture and the atonement (to name but two) are seriously astray.

DOWNES: What would you consider to be the main theological dangers confronting us today and how can we deal with them?

THOMAS: Postmodernity (that spawns post-foundationalism, deconstructionist theologies by the truck load).

The new perspective on Paul which radically reinterprets justification in social and ethnic terms, denying imputation of Christ's righteousness defines a Christian in ecclesiastical rather than soteriological terms.

A hermeneutic of cultural accommodation that questions creational male-female relationships, ecclesiastical vocation and sexual relationships. The denial of penal substitution – a frontal attack on the very heart of the gospel. And much more!

How to deal with them? Pray that God would raise up able theologians to counter this baleful influence. Prayer, prayer and more prayer.

DOWNES: It is natural that a younger generation can find it harder to navigate the theological currents in the church. With all your ministerial experience what advice would you give to younger ministers as they assess and handle various movements today?

THOMAS: Ensure the best theological education. Immerse yourself under warm, sound expository preaching. Develop a theology of the Lord's Day and its accompanying 'means of grace' ministry. Never preach anything that has not withstood the test of time. Read *Dear Timothy: Letters on Pastoral Ministry* (Edited by Thomas K. Ascol, Founders Press).

CHAPTER SEVEN

THE DEFENSE AGAINST THE DARK ARTS

An Interview
with R. Scott Clark

R. Scott Clark is the Associate Professor of Historical and Systematic Theology at Westminster Seminary California, Escondido, California and the Associate Pastor at Oceanside United Reformed Church. He edited and contributed to *Covenant, Justification and Pastoral Ministry* and has written *Recovering the Reformed Confession*.

MARTIN DOWNES: Have you ever been drawn toward any views or movements that time has shown to have been unhelpful or even dangerous theologically?

R. SCOTT CLARK: I didn't become a Christian until my teen years and I didn't join a Reformed congregation until college, so my youth was taken up with the most dangerous positions of all, unbelief and confusion.

I suppose it's politically incorrect for me to call charismatic and pentecostal theology dangerous, but there was a period during my first pastorate where I began to question whether my cessationist views were correct. I spent a fair amount of time praying with some of the folk involved in the Kansas City prophets controversy (though I was quite naïve about what was going on) and reading charismatic literature.

For a time, I was quite drawn to the idea of continuing revelation of the sort advocated by Wayne Grudem. As I worked through his arguments, however, I came to find them unsatisfactory. Ironically, it was hearing him give a paper at the Evangelical Theological Society in Kansas City that really pushed me away from his point of view. Since that time I've come to see how dangerous the idea of continuing revelation (even if one says that it is non-canonical) is and my understanding of the importance of the idea of canon has matured too.

 Ultimately, the idea of continuing revelation is grounded in what I now call the Quest for Illegitimate Religious Experience. It's the fruit of an over-realized eschatology.

DOWNES: How should a minister keep his heart, mind and will from theological error?

CLARK: This is a truly vital question. I am deeply concerned about the number of young, intelligent, but theologically unstable ministers that I see. In many cases it seems that these men are isolated and that they've formed unhealthy friendships that corrupt good morals and theology (1 Cor. 15:33). I know that the relative isolation that I experienced in my first pastorate was part of the way I was tempted toward Pentecostalism. A minister should keep good literary company as well. He must read bad books, as it were, but he must also read good books by reliable authors. We need to query our hearts about why we are drawn to bad company and bad theology in the first place.

Almost invariably I find that those who say that they are 'bored' with orthodoxy don't really understand it. That's the most dangerous place of all: ministers who are badly taught and who've become inoculated against orthodoxy by exposure to a weak strain of it.

The visible, institutional church has the first role in keeping ministers accountable. That's the function of the consistory or session. It's also an important function of other ministers and elders in the broader church (classis and presbytery).

Along those same lines, it is very easy for preparation for preaching and teaching to become mere work. Prayerful study and studious prayer (Warfield) has to be a constant part of the minister's discipline.

It seems clear to me that most of the ministers in Reformed circles who are erring and leading others astray are doing so out of ignorance of the Reformed confessions they have subscribed. Ministers must remember that they are *ministers*. They are not free agents. They have sworn to uphold, defend and teach nothing contrary to the Reformed confessions. They've taken oaths and that requires a certain degree of personal integrity.

Finally, a minister needs to attend to the means of grace. This might sound odd, since the minister's primary vocation is to minister the means of grace to the congregation, but there's so much going on in the minister's head during a service that it's easy to lose track of what's really happening in a service, that God is speaking to His people, that Christ has redeemed His people, and that the Spirit is sanctifying His people through the foolishness of the gospel. The minister must hear the Word himself. He must believe it himself. He must locate himself in the Christian story not only as a worker but as one of the redeemed.

Downes: How have you dealt with church members or students who have been attracted or taken in by false teaching?

Clark: Funny you should ask. I suppose I've been pretty vigorous about it. Some would say 'too vigorous' I'm sure. Some of the students joke that I am a bulldog for orthodoxy. One of the highest compliments I've received in recent years was to be denominated one of 'Machen's Warrior Children'.

In all seriousness, my teacher Derke Bergsma always says, 'Gentlemen, when you go heresy hunting, be sure to use a rifle, not a shotgun.' That's good advice that I haven't always followed as faithfully as I should have done.

When something is public (e.g., a sermon, a book, a lecture), I've spoken publicly. When an issue has arisen in private, I've spoken privately. I've tried to act ecclesiastically, which in our polity is very difficult. I've drafted overtures for the local and regional churches and I try to write, speak and preach as I have opportunity.

Downes: What new errors facing churches today are really contemporary forms of much older false doctrines?

Clark: Virtually everything we face today is a version of something that has occurred before. Open Theism draws from ideas that have been around for centuries. I don't see them interacting seriously with the Christian tradition. Social Trinitarianism runs afoul of the Athanasian Creed. The Federal Vision is, in some ways, a re-hash of Baxter's neonomianism and the eighteenth-century Marrow Controversy.

My impression is that in many cases, the folks who are pushing these errors haven't reckoned with the history of theology or with the Reformed confessions.

Downes: What resources from historical theology are a 'must read' for ministers today to combat them?

Clark: Often in class, when it's appropriate, I simply exposit one or more of the Reformed confessions as an explanation of the Reformed understanding of Scripture. It's amazing how often that seems to help the students. At the end of the day I'm often just a glorified catechism teacher.

As a teacher I naturally think that education is useful. In that regard I guess we live in different worlds. The USA is a very large place with a certain animus against theological education. American Christians tend to be quite activist, placing a low priority on education or even rejecting it altogether.

Even among those who say that they value education, historical education tends to be given short shrift. Our own students are required only to take nine credits (out of 109) of church history. I have only four credits to cover 1000 years of history and theology. For many, that's all the history they'll ever study.

It's not surprising that, when Pelagius or Joachim of Fiore comes knocking, some folks let them in and, in some cases, give them the keys to the kingdom.

DOWNES: Why do old heresies persist?

CLARK: Sin. 'Has God really said?' Calvin is right. 'From this we may gather that man's nature, so to speak, is a perpetual factory of idols' (*Institutes* 1.11.8). After the fall, revealed truth is alien to us. None of us is glorified and thus just as we must continue to struggle against sin because we find it attractive so we continue to struggle against error because we find it attractive. Error often seems 'intuitive' and seems empowering. Truth often seems counter-intuitive and foolish. For example, the way to sanctity is not the law, but the gospel of the cross and the empty tomb. That's not how we think it ought to be. So, the two natures of Christ and the three persons of the deity and sanctification flowing from justification are not how one might expect things to be.

DOWNES: The Westminster Directory of Public Worship has a striking comment, in the section on preaching, about dealing with false doctrine:

> In confutation of false doctrines, he [the preacher] is neither to raise a old heresy from the grave, nor to mention a blasphemous opinion unnecessarily: but, if the people be in danger of an error, he is to confute it soundly, and endeavor to satisfy their judgments and consciences against all objections.

How can this best be applied to pulpit ministry today in relation to the present controversies over justification by faith alone?

CLARK: First, it would help if ministers and elders were acquainted with the historic and confessional doctrine of justification. I find little evidence that most of the proponents of errors under this heading have any real direct knowledge of medieval and Reformation theology. I don't see that they've interacted closely and carefully with the writers of Reformed orthodoxy.

We need as churches to supervise our ministerial students more closely. It sometimes seems as if students go through their studies without sufficient ecclesiastical supervision.

Ministers need to face the Protestant doctrine of justification squarely and ask themselves honestly before God whether they really believe what we confess concerning sin, grace, imputation and faith. Do they really understand what we mean by those words? Is that their faith? If not, they need to reckon with that fact. If they cannot minister honestly and in good conscience under the confessions as a sort of covenant they need to be honest and admit it. Machen made this argument back in 1923 and it's still a sound argument.

I challenge my students every year to an honest self-examination as to whether they really are Protestants and if not, I have a standing offer to help them enroll in the nearest Roman parish or Orthodox catechism class. I respect Francis Beckwith's honesty. It seems pretty clear that he doesn't understand confessional Protestant theology very well, but at least he has been honest enough to admit his disagreement and to act honorably.

DOWNES: How do you cope with men who are sound in many ways, and whose ministries have been beneficial, but who, nonetheless, have held harmful views?

CLARK: This is difficult of course. It's useful to set priorities. For example, it seems clear to me that one's view of the creation days is not of the same order as disagreement over or error on the doctrines of God or justification. So, if a man has useful things to say but errs on a matter that is central to the faith, he should be regarded one way. If he errs on a relatively minor matter, that's another.

Then it depends upon whether and how one has taught the error and to what effect. If a man has come to the New Perspectives or the Federal Vision as if he's reached a great breakthrough and heralds that error far and wide, well, the response should be proportionate. If, on the other hand, an otherwise orthodox pastor stumbles unwittingly into an error, I would deal with him gently.

The response depends upon how one responds. I've had good and useful discussions with men who I thought we're saying problematic things. I've also had some difficult and painful discussions. Sometimes folk respond well, and sometimes they don't. On analogy with church discipline, when one is recalcitrant, the law is in order. When one is penitent, grace is in order.

Usually folk get attention when they move toward heterodoxy, but I'm really impressed with John Piper's honesty and maturity. He realized that his earlier theology was problematic and he spoke up about it. Out of that realization came his recent work on justification. That took courage and integrity.

I guess the main thing is that one has to fear God more than men.

DOWNES: Good men can end up with an excessively negative ministry when they become preoccupied with error. How can a minister keep himself from this temptation?

CLARK: Preach Christ. We have the greatest news to proclaim. If our preaching is tied closely to the text of Scripture and our reading of the text of Scripture is informed by the flow of redemptive history then our preaching will be positive. Yes, we should preach the law in all it's terror, but we should preach the gospel in all its sweetness and glory. If we're preaching Christ from all of Scripture then one can never accuse us of riding a hobby horse.

Paul gives us a great example here. No one was more forceful in confronting error and yet no one was as consistently focused on Christ as our obedient, crucified, resurrected and glorified Savior.

DOWNES: Why has evangelicalism become a haven for theological errors?

CLARK: The short answer is that, since the early eighteenth century, evangelicalism has become synonymous with the Quest for Illegitimate Religious Experience and the Quest for Illegitimate Religious Certainty. These two quests are a sort of Scylla and Charybdis which the Reformation and post-Reformation churches managed to navigate but the modern church has failed to avoid.

Much of this has occurred either because we have over-reacted to Modernity (rejecting electricity because it's associated with that scoundrel Ben Franklin!) or because we have become indentured servants to Modernity. In either case, we're no longer about our own business but attending to another agenda altogether. I'm working on a book on these very topics, so thanks for asking!

DOWNES: In many ways the most significant figure in evangelicalism today is Faustus Socinus. The Socinians were open theists and denied penal substitution and justification by faith alone. Why are these errors, once espoused by the arch-enemies of the Reformation, resurfacing as evangelical options today?

CLARK: Luther identified the two aspects of the theology of glory as rationalism and moralism. Ultimately they coalesce as they have in Socinianism. The initial attraction of the Socinian programme was biblicism - 'Just the Bible ma'am.' It quickly became clear that this naïve biblicism soon was really just a mask for a pernicious rationalism.

Evangelicalism, with its twin poles of QIRC and QIRE is, in too many ways, the step-child of that movement. Moralism is the twin of rationalism. Justification *sola gratia, sola fide* will never satisfy the rationalist (who thinks that he knows what God knows, the way God knows it) any more than the resurrection satisfied the Athenian Philosophical Society. The Socinian offers the same logic as Rome: the way to get folk to behave is to make salvation a *quid pro quo*.

When we divorced ourselves in the eighteenth century from our Reformation roots, we became willing victims of the temptations of the Socinian programme. Modern evangelicalism is not a churchly movement and therefore it's not a confessional movement. It is a pietist movement. It's intentionally trans-denominational. It's intentionally doctrinally minimalist. It's intentionally grounded in religious experience. How could such a movement not become susceptible to any error offering to maximize religious experience and sanctity?

DOWNES: What would you consider to be the main theological dangers confronting us today and how can we deal with them?

CLARK: The definition and nature of the gospel is fundamental to the existence of the Protestant church. It was a Reformed theologian, J. H. Alsted, who said that the doctrine of justification is the article of the standing or falling of the church. In that case, we should attend to the NPP and Federal Vision questions immediately just as a physician would attend to a heart attack immediately.

To torture the metaphor further, it also turns out that the patient has bone cancer and is in desperate need of long term treatment. The patient needs an immediate bone-marrow transplant from Martin Luther and John Calvin. Next, the patient will need after-care provided by Francis Turretin and Johannes Wollebius. Finally, the patient needs to make immediate lifestyle changes. He must stop eating Bill Hybels and the *Purpose Driven Life* for lunch. These are the theological and ecclesiastical equivalents of the worst sort of cholesterol.

The evangelicals (I am evangelical in the same way I am catholic but I'm not 'an evangelical' nor 'a Catholic') need to decide whether they would be Christians in any way recognizable to any previous generation or whether they will continue to careen uncontrollably toward a degree of Narcissism hitherto unknown.

Will the evangelicals settle for being merely Christian? Notice I did not say, 'mere Christian' but *merely* Christian.

By this I mean, will they accept that we live in the inter-regnum and that neither revival nor jihad will bring in the consummation? Only the preaching of the foolishness of the gospel brings the kingdom and then only to the degree that God wills. If they (and the Reformed churches with them) would resign themselves to living ordinarily in the 'in-between' age, a lot of the things that attract them now would lose their luster.

CHAPTER EIGHT

HEROES AND HERETICS

An Interview with Iain D. Campbell

Iain D. Campbell is Pastor of the Free Church of Scotland congregation in Back on the Isle of Lewis. He is the author of *Heroes and Heretics* and *The Doctrine of Sin*.

MARTIN DOWNES: As you reflect back to your days in seminary and early years in the ministry were there men who started out with evangelical convictions who later moved away from the gospel? How did you cope with that?

IAIN D. CAMPBELL: I can think of several colleagues who left the ministry for various reasons; prominent in my mind are men who left the ministry over issues relating to personal relationships and immorality. In the case of the latter, goalposts were widened to allow alternative lifestyles to be tolerated in their own Christian life, and to that extent moved away from the Lordship of Christ in the gospel.

Such movements were very sad, and were damaging to the cause of Christ within the Church. They opened my own mind to the very real danger of heterodoxy and heteropraxy, and suddenly heresy wore human faces.

I suppose one of my ways of coping with this was the realization of the truth of Paul's words in Acts 20:30 where he showed the elders at Miletus that the greatest dangers would arise from within the church rather than come at the church from outside.

DOWNES: Have you ever been drawn toward any views or movements that time has shown to have been unhelpful or even dangerous theologically?

CAMPBELL: Mercifully not. I have continued to preach the Reformed doctrines on which I was reared. I have observed, however, how the apparent deadness of the Reformed church can sometimes lead men to embrace other more exciting ways of doing church. That in my view is often where false teaching comes in: with the application of wrong solutions to the real problem of lack of growth and apparent spiritual vitality.

DOWNES: How should a minister keep his heart, mind and will from theological error?

CAMPBELL: I often reflect on what Dr John Kennedy of Dingwall said in the nineteenth century of the ministers of his generation: that 'each one of them would have been distinguished as a Christian, though he had never been a minister.' That often causes me to reflect on whether my Christianity is in my ministerial office, when my ministerial office should be rooted in my Christianity. That is to say, our relationship with Christ has to be the foundation of our relationship to Christ's people.

So we need to use every means God has given us to feed our own souls. That means at least three things: regular reading of the Bible for ourselves, regular exposure to gospel preaching for ourselves, and regular communion with God. It's often more in the breach than in the observance, but there is no getting away from the fact that our public ministry can only be guarded by our private devotion to Christ.

Having stated the obvious, however, I think there is another factor that has to come in when we are discussing the preacher of the gospel: that is the need to remind ourselves of the limits of our theological position. I think that for this an immersion in the great creeds of the church is indispensable. I regularly read through the Westminster Confession of Faith and its Catechisms, as well as the ancient creeds, just to remind myself that the church has defined its theological position in the past, and that to remain within the limits of orthodoxy is a sure way to guard against error.

I used to think that a minister could not raise his congregation above his own spiritual temperature. I no longer think that. I believe that it is possible for us to enter a pulpit and preach orthodox doctrine with passion, and yet be cold in our love for God and for His people. We need to fill our own souls with the good things of the Word if we are to preach with sincerity and integrity.

DOWNES: Calvin said that ministers have two voices. One is for the sheep and the other for warding off the wolves. How have you struck the right balance in this regard in your pulpit ministry?

CAMPBELL: Have I struck the right balance? Mmm … I suspect that the faithful exposition of the biblical text will give sufficient balance in this regard. By unpacking the meaning of Scripture we will both feed the flock and warn the wolves.

DOWNES: Good men can end up with an excessively negative ministry when they become preoccupied with error. How can a minister keep himself from this temptation?

CAMPBELL: By faithful exposition of the biblical text. Just tell it as it is, and the Word will naturally expose error as it conveys the Truth. Balance is often the missing ingredient in ministry. We cannot allow our own preoccupations to color our exegesis, and we must remain within the limits of Scripture.

By keeping Christ before us as the central theme of all our proclamation and evangelism. It is a sobering test to ask whether Christ has been magnified in our message. He is the Truth, and to preach Him in all the glory of His Person and Work will give our ministry a positive edge.

I think all our preaching must be evaluated by this criterion. We need to preach Christ out of all the Scripture. He will expose error, but He is also the remedy for those who are in error. We are ambassadors of both the word and the Word – the written word is our only access to the incarnate Word. Our preoccupation ought not to be with theological error, but with Christ.

By careful application of the text to the actual needs of the people before us. Indulge me when I quote again from Kennedy of Dingwall (he's one of my heroes!) – he said that the best preachers of Ross-shire were those who aimed to be understood by the 'lowest' minds in their congregations, rather than by the 'highest'. To expose theological error is one thing; but theology was meant for the people of God. Let's make sure we are feeding the people who are actually before us, and not berating those who are not!

By the discipline of trying to summarize our message in one sentence. What will people take away with them? Will their hearts have been warmed in the exposition of the Word, just like the travellers to Emmaus in Luke 24?

DOWNES: How have you dealt with church members or students who have been attracted or taken in by false teaching?

CAMPBELL: By personal counsel, or by church intervention. In some cases there has been a positive response; in other cases people have left for churches and fellowships where their new ideas can be domesticated.

DOWNES: How do you cope with men who are sound in many ways, and whose ministries have been beneficial, but who, nonetheless, have held harmful views?

CAMPBELL: If this refers to historical figures, then I think it is easy enough to use the best of their material and filter out the rest. Tares and wheat grow side by side in the best works, and we can glean the wheat but try to avoid the tares.

I love Spurgeon, but I think he was wrong on baptism. I love Dabney, but I think his views on slavery were distressing. I love Calvin, but I don't countenance his attitude to the burning of Servetus. I love Hodge, but I think he conceded too much to Darwinism. I love Augustine, but I don't go with his high Churchmanship.

Interestingly, I have been asked to speak on Irenaeus, who, to all intents and purposes, was the prince of apologists, and certainly one of the leading theologians of the post-apostolic period. He has some useful insights, and produced timely works. Yet William Cunningham says that he illustrates how quickly the post-New Testament church fell into error.

So we are all learning, and most of us are dwarves trying to stand on giants' shoulders. Sometimes the giants fail us, but they still help us to see further than we could without them.

DOWNES: What would you consider to be the main theological dangers confronting us today and how can we deal with them?

CAMPBELL: I think the devil's twin weapons against the church have been persecution and false doctrine. In places where persecution hits the church, very often it serves to guard the purity of the church's doctrines. In places where it doesn't, the virus of error spreads easily.

I suspect that the church in the Western world is in the latter situation. There is no great persecution; our lives are comfortable, and not the least in danger. So we can easily make room for theological compromise.

I would list the following as some of the main theological dangers facing us:

- The authority of Scripture, and in particular the authority of the Old Testament. The devil has always attacked

God's Word, and has often undermined the authority of the older covenant. As a result we have found common ground with evolutionists, because we are slack on Genesis 1, with liberals, because we have argued that elements of myth found their way into the Bible, and with ecumenists, because we have failed to take seriously the command to Israel to be separate.

- The neglect of God's law, and in particular the abiding relevance of the ten commandments. There has been a huge shift in our understanding of the relationship of law to grace. Whereas before it was a given that the law was the believer's rule of life, that is now characterized as legalism. Christians become obsessed with discovering God's will; yet they often refuse the one rule for living that God intended to be permanent out of all the rules he had given Israel.

- The rejection of the penal subsitution model for understanding the atonement. We have swallowed the lie that this is a Western, legal metaphor, the overemphasis of which has led to a neglect of other models for understanding the atonement. The reality is that this is the only model which allows the other 'models' to work. The church has allowed progressive reinterpretations of the cross to eclipse the central message of the gospel, without which there is no gospel: Christ was made sin for us.

- The reinterpretation of the doctrine of justification as being little more than a new salvation by works. The new perspective on Paul has done untold damage to the cause of the gospel, by de-emphasizing our individual responsibility and recasting our cardinal doctrine.

The only remedy is to continue preaching old truths with the clarity and conviction of our theological forefathers. It is no obscurantism to walk in old paths; and the world needs the old gospel.

DOWNES: It is natural that a younger generation can find it harder to navigate the theological currents in the church. What advice would you give to younger ministers as they assess and handle various movements today?

CAMPBELL: To give a prime place to their reading of Scripture, not to waste too much time reading the literature of the new gurus of theological reflection (don't we support seminaries so that our academics will do that for us?), to test all the spirits, always to be reading Puritan literature, to use every opportunity for fellowship with like-minded ministers who love the truth as it is in Jesus, and to bathe their ministry in prayer.

CHAPTER NINE

THE GOOD SHEPHERD

An Interview
with Dr Tom Ascol

Dr Tom Ascol is Senior Pastor of Grace Baptist Church, Cape Coral, Florida. He serves as the Executive Director of Founders Ministries and editor of the *Founders Journal*. Dr Ascol has edited *Dear Timothy: Letters on Pastoral Ministry*.

MARTIN DOWNES: As you look back over your Christian life and ministry what theological errors has the Lord kept you from?

TOM ASCOL: Early in my Christian life I was greatly attracted to Watchman Nee and the so-called 'Deeper Life' movement. The Keswick view of sanctification held out a vision of the Christian life that I desperately wanted. Such teaching leads either to self-deception in thinking that you have attained it, or to despair in knowing that you have not. By God's grace, the latter was my lot. The discovery of Scripture's teaching on indwelling sin rescued me.

I also was raised with a semi-Pelagian understanding of grace. A person's will was regarded as the key to successful evangelism. I became enamored of psychological techniques that could be employed to motivate people to 'make decisions' for Jesus. The Bible's teaching on sinful human nature and depravity disabused me of that understanding and led me to recognize the sovereignty of God's grace in salvation.

DOWNES: How have you dealt with church members who have become attracted to theological errors?

ASCOL: First and foremost I have tried to emphasize the importance of right doctrine in my regular preaching and teaching. The priority placed on it in Scripture as well as the many warnings of being led astray are regularly highlighted. Sadly, we have had members who have become ensnared by false teaching. I try to persuade them of the error by pressing them to deal with Scripture in its whole. Trusted confessions of faith are helpful at this point. Those members we cannot convince, we leave with a warning and trust them to the Lord. If the error is serious enough, we remove them from membership.

DOWNES: How should a local church, or an association of churches, take seriously Paul's warning that 'Even from your own number men will arise and distort the truth in order to draw away disciples after them' (Acts 20:30)?

ASCOL: Humility demands that no church or association ignore this sober warning. These were elders that, most likely, Paul himself appointed to serve the church in Ephesus. No man, regardless of his gifts or usefulness is immune to the temptation to distort the truth. This is true for church leaders as well as others. A church should be prepared to deal with this, should the need arise. By adopting a fulsome confession of faith and requiring its leaders to adhere sincerely to it, a church will be much better positioned to address this sad situation than if it had no such confession.

DOWNES: How should a minister keep himself from bitterness and pride when engaged in controversy?

ASCOL: First of all, a minister ought to try to avoid controversy. Sadly, there often is a perverse desire to battle that tends to well up in a minister who is fully committed to proclaim and defend the truth of God's Word. When that is coupled with the abundant distortions of truth that prevail today, a man very easily could find himself doing little else than engaging in controversies. A minister must learn to distinguish those hills on which he is prepared to die from all others and choose his battles carefully. Prayer, Scripture and godly counsel help in this effort.

Secondly, a man must recognize that in the heat of any controversy his greatest challenge lies within his own heart. One of the Puritans said that the temptations that accompany controversy are greater than those that accompany women and wine. Bitterness and pride are only two of them. John Bunyan recognized this and addressed it very graphically with his character, Valiant for Truth, in *Pilgrim's Progress*. Study the account of that man's bloody battle and remember that the three enemies that left him bruised and battered all resided within his own soul!

On a practical note, I try to remember that the truth for which I am contending commands me to love the one with whom I contend. It does not matter if he is a Christian brother or not, since Jesus tells us to love even our enemies. If I allow myself to become vengeful or bitter or arrogant toward my disputants then I am violating the very truth which I profess to defend in the controversy. It would be better for me to remain quiet and let others better suited to represent Christ and His cause take up the battle. It would be best for me to become such a person.

Also, I try to remember that in controversies my goal should be to win people and not arguments. It is easy to hang people on their words by pointing out every misstatement and accusing them of meaning what they genuinely did not intend to communicate. If I see something more clearly and accurately than my 'opponent', then it is only by the grace of God and I should not allow myself to believe or act like it is because I am smarter or better in any way than he is.

Finally, I ask my wife and a few trustworthy men to watch me carefully when I am engaged in controversy and to point out to me where I am exhibiting pride, thoughtlessness or lack of love. God has used them to help me see what I would not have seen otherwise.

DOWNES: What practical steps should be taken by preachers to 'watch their life and doctrine closely'?

ASCOL: Recognize that this admonition is given to us for a reason. Every preacher should remember that better men than we will ever be have fallen into grievous sin and error. Ministers need the gospel as much as anyone and we must learn to live by the grace of God in Jesus Christ every day. We need to deal with our sin daily and trust Christ for forgiveness daily. We must fight against every tendency to resign ourselves to professionalism in ministry. As Robert Murray M'Cheyne said, 'My people's greatest need is their pastor's personal holiness.' Dealing daily with our hearts before the Lord is not optional. This work does not compete with my ministry, it is a vital part of my ministry.

Using trustworthy catechisms and confessions can help guard our doctrinal commitments. Such documents are not infallible, but they provide guardrails which we should over-run, if ever, only with great caution and clear biblical warrant.

DOWNES: The New Testament warns us about the subtlety of error. If false teaching isn't always obvious how can we keep ourselves from being deceived?

ASCOL: The best way to avoid being deceived is to be well-grounded in sound doctrine. Becoming vitally connected to a good church is the means which God has provided to ensure this.

DOWNES: Why does God allow His church to be troubled by false teachers?

ASCOL: Deuteronomy 13:1-4 indicates that one purpose false teachers serve is to provide a test for the devotion of God's people. Paul makes a similar point in 1 Corinthians 11:19 when he indicates that factions (heresies) within a church are necessary to prove the faithfulness of genuine followers of Christ.

DOWNES: Have you been surprised that the point of attack in evangelicalism over the last fifteen years has been over doctrines that are central to evangelical orthodoxy?

ASCOL: No. Evangelicalism lost its center long ago in its pursuit of relevance and acceptability to the popular and academic cultures. When the gospel has been forgotten and theology has been marginalized, we should not be surprised to see fundamental doctrines attacked and discarded.

DOWNES: Are the denials of eternal punishment, penal substitution, and justification by faith alone the 'unpaid debts' of the church? Are they a sign that evangelicals did a bad job of teaching these doctrines or is there some other dynamic at work?

ASCOL: I think they are an indication that we have too long assumed that we know what we believe and why. Attacks on such core doctrines as these are a call to re-examine our convictions in the light of the Bible and to decide whether or not we really do believe what we have professed and too often assumed. Of course, while we can never shirk our responsibility in this we must also remember that we have an enemy who is the father of lies and loves to deceive people.

DOWNES: How do you pray for those in error?

ASCOL: I ask the Lord to open their eyes and show them the truth.

DOWNES: Is there a point of no return for those who embrace heresies? What are the signs that this line has been crossed?

ASCOL: I operate on the conviction that as long as there is breath there is hope. If the Lord can save me then I have no reason to believe that anyone is beyond the reach of His grace.

CHAPTER TEN

A DEBTOR TO MERCY ALONE

An Interview
with Dr Guy Waters

Dr Guy Prentiss Waters is Associate Professor of New Testament at Reformed Theological Seminary in Jackson, Mississippi. He has written *Justification and the New Perspective on Paul* and *The Federal Vision and Covenant Theology* as well as being co-editor with Gary L. W. Johnson of the recent volume *By Faith Alone*.

MARTIN DOWNES: Have you ever been drawn toward any views or movements that time has shown to have been unhelpful or even dangerous theologically?

GUY WATERS: I was raised in a mainline liberal church. Shortly after I became a Christian, my boyhood pastor told me that he was a universalist (he believed that every human being is going to be saved). I remember a lot of sermons from the Gospels (especially Jesus' teachings), but very little from the rest of the Bible. We recited the Apostles' and Nicene Creeds, but I had only a foggy understanding of their meaning.

If you had asked me at age twelve why I was a Christian and why I thought that I was going to heaven, I probably would have pointed to my church membership, to my sometime attendance at church services, to my reputation as a 'good kid' in the community, and to my non-rejection of my upbringing. A personal, vital relationship with the Lord Jesus Christ was something for the fundamentalists, but it wasn't for me.

The liberalism in which I had been raised taught me to put my trust and confidence in myself and in my performance. It was natural religion with a Christian veneer, the acceptance of a modified form of the Covenant of Works ('do this and you will live … with a little help from God!').

The Lord was pleased to awaken me and later to convert me. By His grace and mercy, I was confronted with and drawn to biblical truths that I believe were absent from the teaching of my youth (but would have been repugnant to me at that time had I been taught them): the infinite holiness of God, the depth and vileness of my sin, justification by faith alone, and the necessity of regeneration by the Holy Spirit. The Lord has enabled me to grow in my understanding of the Reformed faith, but by God's grace I have not been drawn, for instance, to Arminianism or Roman Catholicism.

DOWNES: How should a minister keep his heart, mind and will from theological error?

WATERS: I think the minister must first convince himself that he is subject to theological error. The deceit and draw of error is no less powerful than it is subtle. The moment we persuade ourselves that we are immunized from theological error is the moment we have opened the gates of our heart to that deadly Trojan horse.

The minister should be constantly studying the Scripture. He should also be reading and studying recognized creeds and confessions, like the Westminster Standards. We don't place the Standards over the Scripture, of course (WCF 1.10). The Standards and other faithful summaries of Christian doctrine allow us, as a friend of mine once put it, to 'check our homework', to compare our studies in the Scripture with those of competent and recognized students of the same.

To this end, the minister should resolve to study good books – the best books. I am amazed when I survey the Internet at both the wealth and poverty of information available there. The web is a dangerous place for someone who is not cultivating the biblical duty of discernment. It is not the 'go to' place for most ministers to advance their theological education after Seminary. The minister should be devouring Calvin, Turretin, the British Puritans, the Dutch 'Second Reformation' Divines, the Scottish and American Presbyterians of the eighteenth and nineteenth centuries, and their modern heirs. The minister should read recent books, but read them with discernment. Most recent books are untested. Reading the older writers appreciatively allows us both to remain in the 'old paths' and to read recent literature without uncritical enthusiasm towards the contemporary.

DOWNES: Gresham Machen once wrote: 'In the field of New Testament there is no place for the weakling. Decisiveness, moral and intellectual, is absolutely required.' Have you found that to be true in your own experience as a student and teacher of New Testament?

WATERS: I love that quote from Machen. He puts it so well. New Testament studies is not a 'lukewarm' discipline. It is burning hot: the integrity, authenticity and credibility of the New Testament as the Word of God; the identity and authority of Jesus Christ; and the very definition of the gospel itself – all hang in the balance. One called to study and to teach the New Testament must resolve to tackle these issues head on.

But it's not enough to face the questions. One must also be prepared to answer them while firmly standing upon the foundation of biblical Christianity. Ministers and teachers are called to pass along the deposit that they have received and not to compromise it. Accommodating that foundation to the latest trends of scholarship – whether it be Historical Jesus scholarship, or the New Perspective on Paul – undercuts the very purpose of the teaching office in the church: 'The things which you have heard from me in the presence of many witnesses, entrust these to faithful men who will be able to teach others also' (2 Tim. 2:2).

DOWNES: Your two books dealing with the New Perspective on Paul and the Federal Vision, as well as being informative, have a polemic purpose to them. What has motivated you in writing them?

WATERS: In both books, my goal was to help ministers, elders, students, and congregants to do two things: (1) to see what proponents of the New Perspective on Paul (NPP) and the Federal Vision (FV) were saying in their own words; and (2) to judge whether the NPP and the FV were compatible with or hostile to Reformed theology.

Both books began as lectures that were delivered for the benefit of ministers and elders within my presbytery (the Mississippi Valley Presbytery [PCA]). Both the NPP and FV were tangibly impacting churches within our presbytery. I was invited to give these lectures because my doctoral work at Duke University had been under one of the leading proponents of the NPP.

I was motivated by a desire to see the gospel of grace proclaimed with biblical integrity and with clarity in the church. Both the NPP and the FV offer us a doctrine of justification that is grounded partly on our obedience. Consequently, there can be no place for preaching such a doctrine in the pulpits and lecterns of the church of Jesus Christ. I have been tremendously encouraged by the growing consensus among the ministers, elders, church courts and educational institutions of the Reformed church that the NPP and the FV are out of accord with the Reformed confessions.

DOWNES: What have you learned from being involved in dealing with controversies?

WATERS: I have learned at least two things. First, controversy is nothing to be relished for its own sake. Controversies can bring out the worst in the church – the devil prowls about, seeking opportunities to tempt us to sin. What's more, the Internet has allowed us to broadcast such sins on an unprecedented scale.

On the other hand, controversy affords an opportunity to the church. The nineteenth century Scottish Presbyterian William Cunningham once commented that controversy gives the church an occasion to attain to greater precision in articulating the doctrines of the Scripture: the writings of perfectly orthodox men prior to a certain controversy lack the crispness that their successors have attained by virtue of that controversy.

In our day, no new ground has been broken (or needs to be broken) on the doctrine of justification. The justification controversy of late should prompt us to appreciate afresh the precision of our fathers and to strive for greater and needed clarity in our own preaching and teaching. I am hopeful that the unpleasantness of recent years will afford the Reformed church an opportunity to communicate the doctrines of grace with scalpel-like accuracy.

DOWNES: How do you keep yourself from treating true and false doctrine in a detached way?

WATERS: I need to remember two things. First, controversy in the church often centers upon the teaching of the Word of God. When we take up the Scripture in any setting, we are taking up the very words of the Almighty. At the Day of Judgment, Christ will hold us accountable for every careless word spoken (Matt. 12:36). James tells us that teachers in the church 'will incur a stricter judgment' (James 3:1). Because we are not handling fallible human opinions, but God's inerrant speech, we must never handle the Bible in a detached way.

Second, men's eternal destinies hang on their reception or rejection of the Word of God. If the watchman is negligent in his proclamation of the Word of God, God will require of him the blood of the one who perishes as a result (Ezek. 3). We have, then, a sacred obligation to teach the whole message of the Bible clearly and precisely.

DOWNES: How have you dealt with church members or students who have been attracted or taken in by false teaching?

WATERS: A minister whom I have long known and respected puts it nicely – our goal is to build consensus around the truth. We are not engaged in a 'win-at-all-costs' argumentative contest. Our goal is to win the person – not at the expense of the truth, but by means of the truth.

To that end, we need to identify the allure of or concern underlying the false teaching in question. Why is that person attracted to a particular unbiblical doctrine? Very often, the individual is reacting against some other error that he has encountered in his past. One error comes to be substituted for another error. For example, individuals rightly concerned with antinomianism or 'easy believism' in the church may very well be tempted to embrace a neonomian doctrine of justification – justification on the basis of our Christian obedience. Individuals rightly concerned with an unwholesomely subjective piety may very well be tempted to assign the sacraments of baptism and the Lord's Supper a central and defining role in the Christian life.

In such a case, we should endeavor to show them the balance of biblical truth. We should show them that the Scripture, rightly understood, addresses their concerns, and addresses those concerns without the liabilities that the errors in question carry.

That having been said, I think we need to be realistic. Error is sin. In my limited experience, I have seen very few in the grip of serious error truly repent of it. We need to pray – for them and for ourselves. We are but instruments in the hands of a sovereign God. Only the Holy Spirit can dispose the heart to receive the truth. This is not to say that we should be slack in our labors. Far from it. Rather, our labors must be accompanied by fervent prayer.

DOWNES: How do you cope with men who are sound in many ways, and whose ministries have been beneficial, but who, nonetheless, have held harmful views?

WATERS: I have heard the late Dr John H. Gerstner quoted as saying that while it is possible for a man to bleed to death from a paper cut, it is not likely. In other words, every deviation from the whole counsel of God is serious and potentially fatal. Some errors, however, are simply more fundamental than others. Some do not strike at the heart of biblical teaching as others do.

A difficult but necessary task is to evaluate a man's ministry by asking certain basic and diagnostic questions: Is this man preaching and teaching the biblical gospel? Would I be comfortable entrusting an unbelieving friend or relative to his presentation of the gospel? Are the doctrines of God, sin, the person and work of Christ, and the Holy Spirit present in his teaching? Are they present in their biblical integrity? Are they present in their proper proportion? Is his teaching free from errors that would fatally compromise the gospel?

If we can answer those questions in the affirmative, then we should be prepared to count these men brethren, to come alongside them, and to assist them in their ministries as much as we are able. This doesn't mean that we pretend that our differences don't exist. Our common commitment to the gospel of Jesus Christ should give us the freedom to engage one another's differences charitably.

DOWNES: What would you consider to be the main theological dangers confronting us today and how can we deal with them?

WATERS: When I look at the evangelical church at the dawn of the twenty-first century, I suppose that I could draw up a list of any number of specific theological dangers that are before us.

My concern, however, transcends those specifics. Let me mention two things. Machen wrote at the dawn of the twentieth century that the great challenge facing the church was 'doctrinal indifferentism'. I am afraid that nearly a century later, that verdict stands. I sense that a generation ago there was a relatively clear theological understanding of what it meant to be an evangelical. I don't think that is true today. Evangelicalism's boundaries strike me as so porous as to admit virtually anything – Roman Catholicism, Mormonism, Postmodernism, and the list goes on. Part of the problem is a prevailing indifference to doctrine or theology. Our culture – in which it is possible to affirm everything and forbidden to deny anything – doesn't make our job any easier. But if we are not a confessing church, then we have forfeited our right to be the church.

A second and related concern is the appeal of the 'cutting edge' within evangelicalism. Biblical doctrine and the Bible's teaching on the Christian life is, at one level, quite boring. It is simple, lacking in gadgetry and spectacle, and unchanging. Whether it is the latest theological 'hand-me-down' from the academy, or the most recent technique or movement for living the Christian life, the church seems to have an unwholesome longing for what is promoted as 'new, fresh and relevant.' Of course, in reality there is nothing new under the sun. 'Fresh' and 'cutting edge' are terms that often mask our ignorance of church history. If we did enough digging, we would find that the church has long ago weighed, tried and discarded most of what is being presented to us as the 'latest thing'. God's admonition is especially timely in our present age: 'Thus says the LORD, "Stand by the ways and see and ask for the ancient paths, where the good way is, and walk in it; and you will find rest for your souls"' (Jer. 6:16).

CHAPTER ELEVEN

TRUTH, ERROR
AND
THE END TIMES

*An Interview
with Kim Riddlebarger*

Dr Kim Riddlebarger is Senior Pastor of Christ Reformed Church in Anaheim, California, and Visiting Professor of systematic theology at Westminster Seminary California, Escondido, California. He is also a co-host of the White Horse Inn radio program. He is the author of *A Case for Amillennialism* and *The Man of Sin*.

MARTIN DOWNES: You have written extensively on eschatology. Why have you focused on this subject?

KIM RIDDLEBARGER: I have been interested in eschatology since I was young. I was one of those kids who built model airplanes, tanks and ships. My folks used to watch Howard C. Estep (from the World Prophetic Ministry) on TV. He would talk about the Arab-Israeli wars (in 1967), and then warn of how US and Soviet arms sales were setting the stage for the rise of the Antichrist, and the battle of Armageddon. Estep would show pictures of all the latest jet fighters and tanks, and then describe how they would produce such carnage that the blood would flow as deep as a horse's bridle (Rev. 14:20). That kind of stuff really fascinated me.

While Estep's TV program may have got me started, one of the first serious theology books I ever read was Hal Lindsey's *Late Great Planet Earth*. I was fourteen at the time (1969), and as a result of reading Lindsey's book over and over again, I was completely hooked on the subject of speculative eschatology. I eventually read most of the leading dispensational writers, including John Walvoord, J. Dwight Pentecost and Charles Ryrie. I even taught dispensational Bible studies at work, and at church, up until my mid-twenties.

As an Arminian dispensational Baptist, my conversion to Reformed theology was a long and painful one – five years, kicking and clawing every step of the way. As I slowly became Reformed, my dispensational eschatology was the last thing to go. So I knew dispensationalism quite well, I understood why people are attracted to it, and I knew its weaknesses.

When the White Horse Inn (the radio show, which I co-host with Michael Horton, Rod Rosenbladt, and Ken Jones) went on the air nearly twenty years ago, many of the callers (the program was originally broadcast live and we took listener calls) asked about how Reformed theology impacted eschatology. Many of these folk were feeling the same tensions I had felt. Since I had worked through many of these same issues, eschatology became a matter of professional interest. So, I sought to prepare a series of lectures and a syllabus on eschatology (from a Reformed amillennial perspective) entitled 'For He Must Reign', which eventually became my book, *A Case for Amillennialism* (Baker, 2003).

Downes: How did you come to an amillennial position on the end times?

Riddlebarger: As I mentioned, this was a long and difficult struggle for me. My family owned a Christian bookstore, so I was raised in the heart of the evangelical subculture. We sold just about every dispensational book imaginable.

One of the young men who delivered our merchandise was a Reformed Christian. He started asking me simple questions about dispensationalism, and it frustrated me to no end that I couldn't answer his questions. The more I would read – with the goal of answering/refuting him – the more questions I had about my own dispensational convictions. Slowly but surely, my dispensationalism began to unravel.

Eventually, I embraced a Reformed soteriology, and attended a local (but now defunct) Christian graduate school (the Simon Greenleaf School of Law) headed by the noted apologist, John Warwick Montgomery. The school offered an M.A. in apologetics – another interest of mine. When I graduated, Dr Montgomery, and my future White Horse Inn compatriot, Dr Rod Rosenbladt, asked me to come back and teach. Both encouraged me to attend the new Reformed seminary in California (now Westminster Seminary California). So, upon Montgomery's recommendation, I enrolled at Westminster in 1981, pretty much as a dispensational, baptistic, five-point Calvinist.

Over the next three years, I drove my professors (Drs Godfrey, Strimple, Kline, and Johnson) crazy with all of my questions.

Reading Vos, Kline, Hoekema, and the rest, continued to chip away at my dispensationalism. Eventually, I gave up the fight and retreated from dispensationalism to historic premillennialism. But that didn't last long. The one book that finally pushed me over the edge was Arthur Lewis' short but powerful book, *The Dark Side of the Millennium*. Lewis showed how difficult it was for premillenarians of any stripe to explain the presence of evil at the end of the millennial age, especially since it was impossible for people to enter the millennial age in natural bodies. When Christ comes back, the only two categories of people are elect/reprobate and sheep/goats. Since there cannot be people on earth in natural bodies after the judgment (Luke 20:34-36, was huge to me in this regard), then who are these people who remain in natural bodies (living next to those who have already been raised), and who supposedly revolt against Christ after Satan is released from the abyss?

To me, this argument rendered all forms of premillennialism completely untenable. Although I flirted with postmillennialism for a time, I became amillennial just about the time I graduated from Westminster in 1984.

DOWNES: I take it that you would consider a dispensational hermeneutic to be an incorrect way to read and understand Scripture. How serious an error would you consider dispensationalism to be?

RIDDLEBARGER: Yes, I consider dispensationalism to be a very problematic way to read Scripture. While dispensationalism is a hermeneutic (despite protests to the contrary), one can be a dispensationlist and a five-point Calvinist. John Nelson Darby and John MacArthur come to mind. But dispensationalism's two interpretive presuppositions (that God has distinct redemptive purposes for Gentiles and national Israel, and that we must interpret biblical prophecy 'literally') are highly problematic. God's redemptive purpose is to save His elect – both Jew and Gentile. This is why there is one gospel, and this is why Paul can tell us that Christ's purpose (under the new covenant) is to make Jew and Gentile one (cf. Eph. 2:11-22). This flies directly in the face of the dispensational hermeneutic which sees one gospel, but distinct redemptive purposes for Jew and Gentile.

And while dispensationalists rail against those who 'spiritualize' the Bible, the amillenarian insists upon interpreting Old Testament prophecy as Jesus and the apostles do. The tough thing for dispensationalists to face is that Jesus and the apostles do the very thing dispensationalists claim should not be done. This means that at the end of the day, it is dispensationalists who don't take the Bible 'literally' since they insist that Old Testament passages which speak about the role of Israel, tell us in advance what the New Testament writers actually mean. This, of course, is highly problematic.

The New Testament writers must be allowed to interpret the Old Testament, especially in light of the coming of Christ.

All of that is to say, dispensationalism certainly does not rise to the level of heresy. But it really does obscure clear passages, and it does not allow us to understand the course of redemptive history as Jesus and the apostles understand it. Ironically, it was the zealots and Pharisees of Jesus' day, who were most angry with Jesus when He told them that the kingdom promises of the Old Testament were realized in Him, and not in a national kingdom, or a restored nation of Israel.

DOWNES: How do you account for the plausibility of dispensationalism?

RIDDLEBARGER: I think there are two main factors here. The first is that the early dispensationalists militantly opposed the higher criticism then coming out of Germany. Along with confessional Protestants (for whom the dispensationalists had little regard), dispensationalists fought for the virgin birth of Christ, the penal-substitutionary atonement, Christ's bodily resurrection, and our Lord's bodily return at the end of the age. The 'we take the Bible literally' defense claimed by dispensationalists, was an effective apologetic against those who were suspicious of the supernatural elements in biblical revelation.

Furthermore, the dispensational stress upon progressive revelation gave them a coherent way (a meta-narrative, if you will) to understand the particulars of the story of redemption. From their vantage point, dispensationalists attempted to claim the high ground as those who alone took Scripture seriously, who funded and supported world missions and evangelism, and who sought to educate Christian young people so as to defend themselves against the spirit of the age. These are all commendable endeavors – although, sadly, the dispensational hermeneutic actually undercuts these very points.

A second factor for the plausibility of dispensationalism is the uncanny ability of dispensational prophecy pundits to relate current events to Bible verses. Whether it be 'peace and then come sudden destruction' (1 Thess. 5:3), or a sensationalized catalogue of the signs of the end taken from Matthew 24, dispensationalists are often masters at making it seem as though any geo-political crisis in the world was actually predicted in the Bible. This gives the dispensationalist a great advantage over those of us who approach Bible prophecy exegetically. I can't get on TV or radio every week, and keep people on the edge of their seats, explaining how what they hear on the news was foretold by Daniel or John.

But then I won't have to get on TV or radio and explain why America's role in Vietnam wasn't a fulfillment of biblical prophecy (I have a John Walvoord lecture on tape entitled 'Vietnam in Bible Prophecy'), nor will I have to explain, as Hal Lindsey was forced to do, why the 'Jupiter effect' (when all of the planets lined up creating an increased gravitational pull upon the earth) did not bring about the cataclysmic earthquakes predicted in the Bible at the time of the end. Reformed amillenarians are primarily concerned with biblical exegesis, not with relating current events to verses wrenched from their contexts.

Downes: What would you consider to be the detrimental effects of these views?

Riddlebarger: On one level, in 2 Peter 3:3 ff., Peter warns of scoffers who will come, mocking Christ's claim to return a second time. Well, it becomes a self-fulfilling prophecy of sorts, when we tie the coming of Christ to passing despots who might bring about the rise of the Antichrist (Michal Gorbachev and Gog and Magog, Saddam Hussein and the rise of Babylon) or to speak of the rise of the EU as the Roman empire *redivivus*, only to have these things come and go, and Christ has still not returned. People scoff, in part, because we give them reasons to scoff. If you look at the recent studies of the effects of dispensationalism upon American culture and politics (i.e., Weber's *On the Road to Armageddon*, or Boyer's

When Time Shall Be No More), it is clear that dispensationalism has had great impact upon a number of aspects of American culture, which only serve to increase the fear and suspicions of those outside the church, who now worry that evangelicals are apocalyptic kooks, or interested in creating a theocracy, neither of which is true.

On a more fundamental and theological level, dispensationalism creates serious problems by not seeing 'covenant' as Scripture's own internal architecture, in having no way to properly distinguish law and gospel (although, many dispensationalists get this right, almost by accident), and by providing no explanation for Christ's active and passive obedience (since the law was for a prior dispensation). Furthermore, since dispensationalism teaches that Christ's offer of a kingdom to Israel was rejected, this almost accidentally led to Christ's death for our sins. What if Israel had embraced Christ's kingdom? In all of these areas, dispensationalism obscures what is clear in Scripture, and creates far more interpretive problems than it solves.

DOWNES: If someone has been taught to read the Scriptures with a dispensational framework where would you begin in helping them to understand the continuity of the covenant of grace and the people of God in the whole Bible? Are there any books or articles that are particularly helpful in this regard?

RIDDLEBARGER: The place to begin is to simply make the determination to give covenant theology and Reformed amillennialism a serious look, from the horse's mouth, so to speak. This means reading Reformed amillennial and covenantal writers first-hand, and not making this determination based upon what you may have heard that amillenarians believe by listening to a dispensationalist.

What strikes me from the recent criticisms of amillennialism from people like John MacArthur (who should know better), is that a straw-man is being attacked and then stomped on as though that ends the discussion. Every dispensationalist who wants to 'refute' amillennialism had better be citing from Horton's *God of Promise*, Hoekema's *Bible and the Future*, Venema's *Promise of the Future*, Beale's commentary on Revelation, and Holwerda's *Jesus and Israel: One Covenant or Two?* But they usually don't – well, Barry Horner's recent book, *Future Israel*, is an exception of sorts. Horner takes me to task for teaching an eschatology which shamelessly recapitulates the errors of Rome (huh?). But more often than not, we get the same re-tread arguments from these men in which I never recognize my own position.

I would recommend that anyone who is interested in these things start by reading three books. Start with Mike Horton's *God of Promise* (Baker, 2006). It is the best treatment of the Reformed covenantal hermeneutic in print. I'd also recommend that people read my *A Case for Amillennialism* (Baker, 2003), in which I write for a dispensationalist who is beginning to think about these matters. I'd then recommend Hoekema's *The Bible and the Future* (Eerdmans), for a more comprehensive treatment of Reformed amillennialism.

The hardest part about this for someone who is a dispensationalist is tackling these matters with an open mind. People in dispensational circles have heard so many bad things about amillennialism that it is hard to get a fair hearing. They've been told amillenarians 'spiritualize' the Bible, that we hold to nothing but warmed-over Romanism, and that we 'replace' Israel with the church. None of these things are true. That is incredibly frustrating. Maybe the loud and instantaneous flack that John MacArthur got after his recent 'Shepherd's Conference' speech is an indication that the tables may have turned.

DOWNES: What aspects of eschatology do you consider to be neglected in preaching and publishing today?

RIDDLEBARGER: One thing I would encourage ministers to do is to preach through the book of Revelation (expositionally). This is the last letter written to the churches included in the canon, and it is wonderfully Christ-centered. There are so many good Reformed amillennial commentaries on Revelation now available (Beale, Johnson, Kistemaker, Poythress) that ministers will find much help in avoiding the speculative nonsense, while showing forth the glories of Christ, who, by the way, wins in the end!

I think today's Christians are very well served by the publishers when it comes to eschatology. For every dispensational book, there is a good Reformed amillennial equivalent. That was not always the case.

DOWNES: What views on eschatology lie within the bounds of orthodoxy and what views are out of bounds?

RIDDLEBARGER: I've already addressed my concerns about dispensationalism and premillennialism above. Certainly progressive dispensationalism is a step in the right direction, and I have always had much respect for George Ladd and his variety of historic premillennialism. Since amillennialism and postmillennialism are very similar (in terms of their overall structure) the main difference has to do with the nature and character of the present age. Will there be a golden age before Christ comes back (as in postmillennialism), or is this the age of the church militant upon the earth (as in amillennialism)? While I think the charge that postmillenarians are optimists and amillenarians are pessimists is grossly overblown, that debate tends to be an in-house debate among the Reformed.

While the so-called 'partial preterists' are fully orthodox, 'full' or 'hyper' preterists are not. Those who teach that Jesus' return to Jerusalem in A.D. 70 was the final judgment and the resurrection, deny both the bodily resurrection and the bodily return of Christ at the end of the age. 'Full' or 'Hyper' preterism is heretical and cannot be held by any orthodox Christian – Reformed or otherwise.

DOWNES: What do you think drives people to embrace errors in their thinking about eschatology?

RIDDLEBARGER: One thing, I think, has to do with the same reason people go to fortune tellers. We all want to know what the future holds. We are all curious about what God has in store for us. That is the one hook deep within each of us which gives the prophecy pundits an 'in'. Indeed, the person who can explain how the tragedy on tonight's news was predicted by the Bible, will certainly attract a large audience and sell many books. It makes the Bible seem relevant and it gives a heightened sense of urgency to missions, evangelism, etc. People naturally gravitate toward the sensational, especially if it is thought to impact them. There are always itching ears and people willing to scratch them.

Another reason (and one that is much tougher to deal with) why people embrace error, is that people often have deeply held (and implicit) presuppositions. Many people simply accept what they were first taught, and that is the end of the story. It is hard to get such folk to admit they might be wrong. It's just easier to be wrong and not have to think about it. Dispensationalists are not wrong because they are stupid, but because their starting point and methodology are incorrect. But, then, how do you get people to step back from deeply held beliefs? That is not easy.

This is why both dispensationalists and Reformed amillenarians need to be very candid and reflective about their operating assumptions and presuppositions. We must constantly be willing to check these things in the light of Scripture, and through the refining fire of debating (in charity) those who hold conflicting views.

DOWNES: Given the variety of views on the millennium, and well respected preachers who hold to these views, it can be daunting for church members to be sure that there is a right view and that they can hold to it with confidence. Where should church members start in their thinking about these issues in order to arrive at as clear an understanding of Scripture as they can?

RIDDLEBARGER: Well, since I am in a confessional church (URCNA), I would tell my own church members to start with our own official doctrine. I don't believe our confessions (*the Heidelberg Catechism, the Belgic Confession, and the Canons of Dort*) are infallible, or the final word on every issue, but I do think they very effectively summarize the biblical teaching on many of these doctrines and controversies, including eschatology.

I would recommend that people read widely on both sides of the issue, ask a lot of questions of respected pastors and scholars, and through the process of iron sharpening iron, the truth will eventually become clear. It is important to remember that these differences of opinion exist between us because we are all sinners, not because God's word is unclear.

For those with robust consciences (who don't struggle with the assurance of their salvation, and who don't find the differences among Christians on this topic to be a threat to their own faith), I would also recommend reading the 'debate' books on this topic. Start with Clouse's *Meaning of the Millennium* (IVP), or *Three Views of the Millennium* (Zondervan), edited by Bock. In both of these books an author presents his case, and then the other contributors respond. I find them very helpful.

DOWNES: As the well known saying puts it there should be 'in essentials unity, in non-essentials liberty, and in all things charity' How does this apply to disagreements on the end times among those who would be agreed on the person and work of Christ?

RIDDLEBARGER: It is a great statement, but not always put into practice. For one thing we all need to actually read and interact with the arguments raised by those on the other side, and not stoop to logical fallacies or generalization and *ad hominem* attack. I, for one, have been on the receiving side of this too many times. Don't tell me I'm shamefully regurgitating the errors of Rome. Show me from Scripture why my argument doesn't hold. Chances are, I'll be more willing to listen.

We also need to realize that people hold various views for different reasons, and we need to assume the best of them

– that this is a matter of genuine conviction, not ignorance. The ninth commandment exhorts us to do this.

Reading and understanding the other side's arguments actually help foster respect and clarify where the actual differences are. That is a very helpful process. It is one thing to interact with what you've heard someone say about someone else, as opposed to interacting the person directly.

Dispensationalists, progressive dispensationalists, and historic premillenarians who trust in Christ are Christians, and need to be treated with courtesy and respect. I think John MacArthur is flat-out wrong on eschatology, but since he defends the doctrine of justification by grace alone, through faith alone, on account of Christ alone, then he is my brother. I need to remember that as I interact with him. I urge dispensationalists to do likewise.

But this charity does not apply with full-preterists. They spread a dangerous heresy and must be urged to repent.

DOWNES: How should disagreements on aspects of end times thinking be handled in the context of the local church?

RIDDLEBARGER: Again, as part of a confessional church, this is spelled-out for our church members in our church order (our constitution). It falls to the officers of the local church to deal with these matters on a case by case basis, applying all charity and discernment, yet not allowing the church to tolerate error.

Individual Christians also need to be aware of the fact that if they come to a different view on eschatology than the church they attend, it is not their mission in life to convert the church, or its members to their own view. They need to work with those whom God has placed over them, be patient and teachable. At the end of the day, should they be convinced that they are right and the church is wrong, then the onus is on them to find a church where they feel more comfortable with the doctrine.

Chapter Twelve

FULFILL YOUR MINISTRY

An Interview
with Ron Gleason

Dr Ron Gleason is Pastor of Grace Presbyterian Church (PCA), Yorba Linda, California. He has co-edited, along with Gary L.W. Johnson, *Reforming or Conforming? Post-Conservative Evangelicals and the Emerging Church.*

MARTIN DOWNES: What are the signs of spiritual and theological decline in a minister?

RON GLEASON: Typically, these are little different in a minister or a layperson. Spiritual decline manifests itself in a lack of interest in the things of God; in the means of grace. If I am not reading the Bible *daily* for *myself* that should be a good and clear indicator to me that something is seriously awry. Allow me to elaborate just a little bit on what I just said.

One of the subtleties of the pastoral ministries is that we get involved in our exegesis and sermon preparation and can be lulled into thinking that simply because we are dealing with Scripture for our sermons that that is sufficient. Nothing could be farther from the truth. The same could be said about when/if we visit our members in their homes. There we pray with them and read the Bible with them, but that is still not sufficient for our personal walk with God. We must be reading daily for ourselves. The same is true of prayer. If we exhort and encourage our congregants to pray daily and we're not taking time to go into the private place to pray (cf. Matt. 6:6) then we are not only being hypocritical, but we are robbing ourselves of spiritual blessings.

As far as theological decline is concerned, I believe this can happen with pastors who simply do not discipline themselves to keep up with the theological dangers that present themselves to the Church. A recent example that comes to mind is a colleague asking me to explain the tenets of the Federal Vision, New Perspective on Paul, the theology of Norman Shepherd, and the Emergent Conversation to him. Granted, we can't know everything about these movements, but as long as they have been viable options for some misguided folk, we ought to be able to give a general outline of the movements along with some salient points about their respective dangers.

DOWNES: Paul told the Corinthians that stewards of the mysteries of God should be found trustworthy. How should a minister put this into practice so that he will be faithful to God in the course of his pastoral ministry?

GLEASON: To my mind, far too many ministers today place too much of a premium on peripheral matters. That is to say, they become entangled in minor matters to the neglect of the most important aspects and facets of pastoral ministry. Being found trustworthy can mean quite a few things, but let me enumerate a few essential components of a faithful ministry. First, is the attention he pays to preparing the weekly sermon(s). A faithful minister doesn't go to this or that web site (you know, a popular pastor) and semi-plagiarize what he can download there. He painstakingly wrestles with the text and faithfully preaches what the text says. Far too many of us have sat in congregations where the pastor used a text for a mere pretext. He had something that he wanted to say – maybe something in a pop-psychology or political book he read – and a text is found that *somehow* expresses what he wants to say, so he uses it, never intending to expound on what the text says.

A minister should be trustworthy in his teaching. I delight and rejoice to teach my congregation. There are some pastors, however, who find this a burden. Perhaps this is a 'generational' thing, but I find a number of younger pastors lazy. If the congregation reaches a size of 150, then they think it's time to hire someone else to help them. Other young pastors have told me that they refuse to preach and teach on the same day. What?! This kind of Perfume Prince mentality stinks in the world and it reeks even worse in the church.

Faithful ministers visit the sick and shut-ins, conduct the necessary meetings, counseling, and take care of their administrative tasks as well. The sign of a trustworthy pastor is not the size of his congregation, but in his dedication to the people with whom God has entrusted him.

DOWNES: Why do confessional denominations requiring subscription become infected with error and change theologically?

GLEASON: In general I believe the answer has to do with a form of cowardice. Friends either see or hear friends changing their views and are reticent to say anything. The short answer is that if I 'sign on the dotted line' to be Presbyterian – which I have – then I have a moral responsibility to maintain, fully espouse and enthusiastically teach what I've given my word that I think is true, right and good. In my church – the PCA – I took a vow that if, at any time, my views changed, I would, of my own initiative, make those changes known to my Presbytery. I believe that I have a number of colleagues who are ethically remiss in that department.

The changes occur and the damage is done when we become 'men-pleasers' rather than remaining God-pleasers.

DOWNES: Once this kind of decline sets in can it be reversed?

GLEASON: Theoretically, yes, but historically the answer has been no. Of course it depends on the degree of decline, but once you've started down the proverbial slippery slope, it's next to impossible to find the brakes. I've been accused of holding to 'domino' and 'conspiracy' theories, but more often than not I'm correct not because I'm so insightful and profound, but because there is a history that can be traced. When I was a student and later a pastor in Holland I watched a solid Reformed church gradually disintegrate. How did that occur? It began with wanting women Deacons. Two years later, the issue was women Elders. The next year it was female pastors. When I left in 1984 it was the ordination of homosexuals. Ironically, the same pattern followed me to Canada where in a very short expanse of time the Christian Reformed Church followed suit.

Liberals are tenacious and conservatives are cowards, always wanting to be nice guys. The case of Charles Hodge and Charles Finney is a classic case in point. We fail to see that the denomination we may love is under attack and quite often the matter seems so innocent and insignificant, until one morning we wake up and no longer recognize our church.

DOWNES: Is there greater danger from openly, and aggressively, unorthodox preachers in a denomination or from the people who want to keep organizational unity?

GLEASON: I think it's hard to pin this one down, primarily because both are insidious. For example, in the PCUSA there are open, aggressive, agenda-driven feminists who are a huge danger. At the same time, we must also be on our guard for the 'iron fist in the velvet glove' that comes from Mr Nice Guy. I have witnessed both. Referring back to my comments about cowardice, I've noticed that if you attempt to confront Mr Nice Guy, you turn into the town bigot in the eyes of some. My response, however, is: so be it. History points us to the irrefutable fact that both the openly aggressive as well as the quiet agenda-driven folk are detrimental.

DOWNES: Many evangelicals take a minimalist view of doctrinal statements. What are the benefits of making use of a fuller confession?

GLEASON: It's far better – and more honest – to lay your cards on the table at the outset. Eventually, if you have any conscience and scruples at all, you're going to have to get around to telling them the truth anyway. One of the things we make known during our New Member's class is where we stand on worship, confession, preaching, fellowship, tithing, and a host of other matters. We do have members who are not truly Presbyterian, but we make it known to them that they may not teach or be leaders, even though they are considered communicant members. Some leave; some stay. That's life.

DOWNES: How should a church make the most of the Reformed confessional heritage, especially if this has become neglected or unknown?

GLEASON: Preach it, teach it, and show the members that you are not ashamed to be who and what you are. Those who are truly Reformed/Presbyterian should be comfortable in their ecclesiastical skin. If the heritage has been neglected, get it out of the closet, dust it off, and start showing everyone how lovely and helpful it is for all of life. Let them see how knowing these things is a true aid and benefit to and for the Christian life and not something to be ashamed of. Teach your people why it is both important and helpful to be able to rely on historical documents that are so in concert with Scripture and that often put complicated, different matters into simple terms that even children can grasp the significance.

DOWNES: How should a minister make the most of the same in his devotional life and in his teaching?

GLEASON: I'll begin with the last first. In his teaching, he can take the time to show how our confessional heritage summarizes key doctrines for us. In addition, he can take the time to walk the congregation through these documents. Personally, I've put together workbooks on these documents. I have a two-volume, 400-page workbook on the Heidelberg Catechism and a 200+ page workbook on the Westminster Shorter Catechism. I have workbooks on prayer and the Ten Commandments, both of which make use of the Heidelberg Catechism and the Westminster Standards.

In my devotional life I find memorization of Scripture and the confessions goes hand in hand. My first reliance is upon Scripture, but choosing a good confession can be helpful. I think there are few better human explanations of the biblical doctrine of regeneration than the one found in the *Canons of Dort*. These documents are a spiritual treasure trove for the wise pastor, church leader, and congregant.

DOWNES: How can the danger of the secondary standard becoming better known than the Bible be overcome?

GLEASON: The best and easiest way is to keep reiterating what the Westminster Confession of Faith (1.4) and the Belgic Confession (Article 7: *The Sufficiency of the Holy Scriptures to be the Only Rule of Faith*) say. The first and primary means of grace is the Word of God. We begin there and we constantly return there. We show how serious theologians have led us there and have spoken of their own writings and confessions as secondary and fallible. Nonetheless, our confessional heritage is an adequate and reliable summary of what Scripture teaches.

DOWNES: What are the most encouraging signs of spiritual life and theological stability in the contemporary church scene?

GLEASON: As odd as this may sound, I'm convinced that the most encouraging signs of spiritual life are found in churches that read the Bible, preach the Bible, pray the Bible and sing the Bible. These are also the most theologically stable in that they are not constantly trying to 'fudge' or 'renege' on what they say they believe. They are simply up-front about their core beliefs. The pastors preach expository sermons and feed the people of God on the other means of grace that God has so graciously provided.

DOWNES: You are known for your deep interest in the writings of Herman Bavinck. How can his work help us with some of the challenges and dangers that we face today?

GLEASON: Bavinck's works are 'timeless' because he always wrote in concert with Scripture. This is not to suggest that Bavinck was infallible, but he was a man thoroughly conversant with the Word of God and his writings reflect a solid acquaintance with the Bible. It should come as no surprise that many of the theological situations of Bavinck's day (Moralism, Existentialism, Relativism, Mysticism, Subjectivism) are alive and well today. In each paragraph Bavinck provides his reader with an historical examination of the subject, thorough biblical exegesis, and a plain exposition of the matter under discussion. Many theologians today fail to recognize old heresies in their new garb. Therefore, mastery of the contents of Scripture, thorough acquaintance with a number of Reformed/Presbyterian confessions, and reading such a rock-solid man as Herman Bavinck can only serve to benefit the Christian.

CHAPTER THIRTEEN

THE FIGHT OF FAITH

An Interview
with Sean Michael Lucas

Sean Michael Lucas is Senior Pastor of First Presbyterian Church, Hattiesburg, Mississippi. Previously he was Vice-President for Academics and Assistant Professor of Church History at Covenant Theological Seminary, St. Louis, Missouri. He has written *Robert Lewis Dabney: A Southern Presbyterian Life*, *On Being Presbyterian*, and is the co-editor, along with Robert Peterson, of *All for Jesus*.

MARTIN DOWNES: What are the signs of spiritual and theological decline in a minister?

SEAN MICHAEL LUCAS: Ultimately, I think that the root of ministerial decline is the loss of a genuine communion with the Triune God that is rooted in Holy Scripture. When we cease to believe, know and experience deeply that God's steadfast love is better than life (Ps. 63:3) and that knowing Christ surpasses all other things in our lives (Phil. 3:8), then it seems inevitable that spiritual decline will start to set in. That is why the Christian life is a fight of faith and, as John Piper puts it, a fight for joy.

For most of us, perhaps spiritual decline sets in in two ways. First, we come to believe that the busy-ness of our ministries demands that we spend our time trouble-shooting spiritual problems rather than pursuing the 'one thing needful' (Luke 10:42). This is tied together with the second issue, which is that we truly believe that this ministry is our ministry, rather than Jesus' own ministry to His people which He performs through us.

After all, if this is my ministry, then I cannot slumber nor sleep; I must keep running and gunning, moving people to the right spots and manipulating spiritual change. But if this is Jesus' ministry, then my highest priority must be living in genuine communion with Jesus, delighting and satisfying myself in Him in such a way that I am utterly reliant upon Him to do His work among His people in His power for His glory. I must live in such a way that I know, deeply and experientially, that the 'battle is the Lord's.'

And the way this dependent living happens is by daily worshipping God through His Word. Each morning as I come to worship God through His Word, I am begging Him to stir my heart's affections through His Word to pursue Him that I may gain Christ – to find Jesus of such surpassing worth that I'm willing to count ministry, family and life itself to be an utter loss in comparison to Him. And so, Jesus' Spirit uses His Word to open the eyes of my heart to see Christ's glory and to give myself over to Him.

Now, we tend to think that the reasons for spiritual decline are, well, spiritual and the reasons for theological decline are theological. However, I think the cause of theological decline among ministers is the same: a failure to meditate deeply and meaningfully on the fact that God Himself is the glory of the gospel and that my very life is tied up with communion with the resurrected and ascended Christ by Word and Spirit.

In place of this vital communion, ministers will tend to focus on social ministries, on relevancy, on community. Such in turn leads to all sorts of questions of the Bible's own teachings

– after all, if one wants to be relevant, then can't we simply ignore or deny the Bible's teaching about inerrancy? About the effect of the Cross? About the nature of the resurrection? About the roles of women in church and home?

It must be said that a desire for mercy and justice, for cultural transformation, and genuine community are proper in their place, but if they are not rooted in a prior individual, vital communion with God through Christ by the Spirit in the Word, then they will finally lead to moralism and theological decline. *At the heart of theological decline is the reversal of the indicative and imperative* – in place of genuine communion with the living God rooted in our union with Christ, ministers substitute cultural relevance, social impact, and global transformation through good deeds.

Downes: Why do confessional denominations requiring sub-scription become infected with error and change theologically?

Lucas: Back in the 1720s, as American Presbyterians battled over whether they should require doctrinal subscription, the two titans who argued about it publicly were John Thomson and Jonathan Dickinson. To boil their arguments down, Thomson believed that without some doctrinal standard, it would be hard to investigate the theological views of new ministers in a way with which everyone would agree and which would preserve orthodoxy; Dickinson suggested that doctrinal standards could not actually prevent heresy and that the only hope was a genuine experience of the New Birth.

One of the little recognized points that resulted from the 1729 'Adopting Act', in which American Presbyterians adopted the Westminster Standards as their doctrinal rule, was that the church essentially said that both Thomson and Dickinson were right. In order for a church communion to maintain the course, there needed to be doctrinal standards to which ministers subscribed and there needed to be genuine spiritual life that would affirm the subscribed-to doctrinal truths. These two 'sides' needed to be held together.

It strikes me that when confessional denominations lose their way, they do so when one side or the other is denied. And so, for American mainline Presbyterians in the middle of the twentieth century, there was extreme discomfort with the sense that there should be a single doctrinal standard, period. Subscription to the Standards was weakened first through doctrinal revision (in the north in 1903 and in the south in 1941), then through the 1924 Auburn Affirmation which suggested that a variety of interpretations of key doctrines was allowable, and finally through the creation of a book of confessions and a new ordination vow in which the minister promised to be 'guided' theologically by the confessions.

In denying, if you will, the Thomson side – that doctrinal standards are important and necessary for theological purity – mainline Presbyterians affirmed theological pluralism and lost their sense of identity.

On the other side, it strikes me that the other lesson of the American mainline Presbyterians in that period was the loss of genuine piety. In the quest to be culturally relevant, to transform culture, and to engage in social reform, the idea that men and women needed to be 'born again' was an affront. The real problem, they argued, was not sin, but ignorance; and so, the real solution was not evangelism, but education. When Billy Graham appeared on the scene in the 1940s and 1950s, he was opposed as much because he appeared to be 'retrograde' as anything – harping on 'fundamentalist' views of sin and salvation. And yet, Graham and his supporters, both in Presbyterian and other evangelical circles, recognized that unless God transformed people by granting them salvation, theological orthodoxy would not be preserved and ultimately would not count for much.

In denying, if you will, the Dickinson side – that spiritual life is important and necessary for theological orthodoxy – mainline Presbyterians moved the gospel in directions that were ultimately destructive to the faith.

And so, both the Thomson and the Dickinson sides (or the 'Old' and 'New Sides' as the labels of the day went) are necessary for a confessional denomination to remain true to its doctrinal commitments.

Downes: Is there greater danger from openly, and aggressively, unorthodox preachers in a denomination or from the people who want to keep organizational unity?

Lucas: Actually, I do not believe either of these represents the greatest danger to denominations. The greatest danger comes from those who are simply not willing to be troubled to care about the denomination, who are content in their own smaller networks (whether formal presbyteries or informal affinity groups), and who will not engage in the issues of the day.

While one might suggest that the way the fundamentalist-modernist controversy of the 1920s played out was the result of those who sought to maintain unity around denominational programs rather than doctrinal truths (as William J. Weston and Bradley J. Longfield both suggested for Presbyterians), the reality is that there is not such loyalty to denominations today. In fact, those with fundamentalist or evangelical heritages have emphasized the 'inevitable' downgrade of denominations to such a degree that it is very difficult to encourage people that connectional denominations are worth the hassle.

And so, that is why I believe that utter indifference to the plight of denominations is the major danger we face today. Because when doctrinal challenges do come from ministers who are doctrinal, deviant, many ministers, elders and laypeople simply tell themselves, 'Well, it doesn't matter; we can do our own thing over here, use the denomination as a branding and credentialing agency, and not be affected.' Meanwhile, important biblical truths to which God calls us to witness are being questioned in our churches and among our young people.

Downes: Many evangelicals take a minimalist view of doctrinal statements. What are the benefits of making use of a fuller confession?

LUCAS: The reason that evangelicals adopted a minimalist creed was in an effort to unite brothers and sisters across a wide range of denominational backgrounds. These doctrinal statements were first used by organizations like the Niagara Conference on Biblical Prophecy or the World's Christian Fundamentals Association as attempts to broker conservative ecumenism. Of course, these organizations operated in an era when denominational labels signaled deeper biblical and theological distinctions that forged primary religious identity.

Over the past twenty or thirty years, however, these minimalist creeds have served as the doctrinal statements for individual churches and associations of churches in ways that suggest ten or twelve points of biblical truth were all that was necessary for Christian fellowship and identity. And yet, the irony is that these ten-point creeds are not able to do what they promise – because it is always the unwritten creed that operates in a more powerful and exclusionary fashion than the written creeds.

One example of this might be drawn from my alma mater, Bob Jones University, a fundamentalist college in South Carolina. At every chapel service students still recite the University Creed, a doctrinal statement of about ten points. As far as it goes, it is a solid statement of evangelical truths; and for a school that was founded to unite conservative Methodists, Baptists and Presbyterians, it is appropriate. However, at various points in the school's history, there has been discomfort with various aspects of the Reformed faith, whether the doctrines of grace, Covenant Theology, or infant baptism, none of which is addressed in the University Creed. It is an 'unwritten creed' that ends up preventing unity.

The flip side of all this is that more detailed confessional statements should provide greater unity. It is striking to me that several places in the New Testament where it appears that early creedal statements are being developed and used (e.g., Phil. 2:5-11; 1 Tim. 3:16), these statements are actually fairly detailed when it comes to core Christological truths. And that is because the church had to maintain unity on the core of their faith – who Jesus was, what He came to do, what He continues to do at the right hand of the Father, what He will do at the end of the age. Unity can only be maintained when the boundaries are clearly set between truth and error.

Even more, fuller confessional statements represent a type of doctrinal advance. As J. Gresham Machen once noted, 'All real doctrinal advance proceeds in the direction of greater precision and fullness of doctrinal statement.' That is why the church did not stop with the first Nicene Creed in 325, for example. While having a wonderful statement of Christological truths, that first Nicene Creed was woefully inadequate on the doctrine of the Holy Spirit. And so, in 381, the Council of Constantinople revised the Nicene Creed to fill out the doctrine of the Spirit (and Gregory of Nyssa felt that the Council did not go far enough in spelling out the deity of the Holy Spirit). More truth will lead to greater precision which should lead to longer confessional statements.

Which is all to say that the move of many evangelicals toward minimalistic creeds is actually a move in the wrong direction. Rather than representing doctrinal advance or even means for unity, minimalistic confessional statements actually lead to doctrinal pluralism, theological downgrade, and suspicion leading to division. Better to have fuller confessional standards and allow differences among believers to be owned manfully and discussed charitably.

DOWNES: Nevertheless fuller confessions don't prevent false teachers from arising within and infiltrating churches. Why is this?

LUCAS: There are a number of reasons why false teachers arise within churches. One reason that we do not think about often is that God is testing His people through the false teacher: 'If a prophet or a dreamer of dreams arises among you and gives you a sign or a wonder, and the sign or wonder that he tells you comes to pass, and if he says, "Let us go after other gods," which you have not known, "and let us serve them," you shall not listen to the words of that prophet or that dreamer of dreams. For the Lord your God is testing you, to know whether you love the Lord your God with all your heart and with all your soul' (Deut. 13:1-3). Perhaps one of the questions that we would do well to ponder in times of doctrinal challenge could be this: will church members love God and His Word more or will they love the new insights of the 'prophet' or 'dreamer'?

Another reason that false teachers arise within churches is that they are often powerful personalities, able to flatter others and to draw a following after them. Paul notes this in Galatians 4:17: 'They make much of you, but for no good purpose. They want to shut you out, that you may make much of them.' Once they draw a crowd, they introduce their 'new' teachings subtly. For example, Peter warns false teachers 'will secretly bring in destructive heresies' and cause many to 'follow their shameful ways' by exploiting them (2 Pet. 2:1-2). And Paul noted to Timothy that 'certain persons, by swerving from these, have wandered away into vain discussion, desiring to be teachers of the law, without understanding what they are saying or the things about which they make confident assertions' (1 Tim. 1:6-7).

The upshot is that false teachers – perhaps sent by God to test, perhaps sent by the devil to destroy – will inevitably claim that they are representing some 'new' biblical truth. They inevitably will pit their new biblical truth against the age-old ways of understanding Scripture (perhaps even claiming that this is 'new light' shining from the pages of the Bible). And they inevitably will lead people astray from the truth of God.

And confessional statements alone cannot prevent false teachers from coming from within and harming God's people. Biblical truth must be coupled together with ministers and elders alert and determined to perform their overseeing role in caring for God's church. This is what Paul commanded the Ephesian elders to do: 'Pay careful attention to yourselves and to all the flock, in which the Holy Spirit has made you overseers, to care for the church of God, which He obtained with His own blood. I know that after my departure fierce wolves will come in among you, not sparing the flock; and from among your own selves will arise men speaking twisted things, to draw away the disciples after them. Therefore be alert' (Acts 20:28-31).

The only way ministers will be committed enough to stand firm in this way will be if they have an eye full of God's glory and grace, which returns us back to the point about vital communion with the Triune God through the Word of God.

DOWNES: As a church historian what would you say are the biggest lessons that we need to learn today from the conflicts in the Presbyterian church caused by liberal theology in the 1920s and 30s?

LUCAS: I've already touched some on this, but it might be good to touch on it a little more. One thing that jumps immediately to mind is how little church leaders at the time, and even in our own day, truly understand the 'genius' of theological liberalism.

Most of us were trained to believe that at the heart of theological liberalism was a denial of the inerrancy of Scripture. But that is not the case. Rather, the heart of theological liberalism consisted of two commitments: first, an epistemological commitment that separated 'religious ways' of knowing from 'scientific ways' of knowing; and second, a willingness to adapt (or correlate) religion to cultural realities.

As a result, as modernist Shailer Matthews noted, theological liberalism was more an attitude than a particular set of doctrinal commitments – an attitude about knowledge and religion's task that moved liberalism in a different direction from traditional Christianity. This attitude allowed theological liberals to exert a wide influence on American intellectual culture for most of the twentieth century.

All that means is that most Christians, both in the 1920s and today, are ill-equipped actually to recognize the pathway on which theological liberals trod. When we suggest that cultural norms raise different questions than in previous centuries, and hence demand different answers on the matters of sin and salvation; or when we pit the human aspects of biblical literature against its divine inspiration in ways that are invidious to the latter; or when we pit biblical and theological language against each other in such a way that suggests 'ordinary' biblical language is more 'real' (and hence, true) than the technical, second-order theological language; or when we suggest that the actual categories of the Bible are actually corporate and not individual, which helps us to provide a relevant message to today's over-individualized Western culture – then, perhaps, we may be moving in directions that are similar to the previous generation's theological liberals. If nothing else, we are proceeding in directions that are less than helpful to biblical Christianity as represented in the Westminster Standards.

Another lesson that could be mentioned is that it is much easier to cobble together a coalition that is against whatever is the issue of the day, than it is to present a positive witness to the world. I think of that lesson from the sad story of J. Gresham Machen, Carl McIntire, and the Division of 1937, which created the Orthodox and Bible Presbyterian Churches. While Machen's witness was undoubtedly necessary, and while the brave northern Presbyterians who stood with him were heroic in their stand for the truth, the quick demise of the initial 'Presbyterian Church of America' after eighteen months pointed out that fundamentalism – a willingness to separate from error – was much easier than biblical Presbyterianism – a connectional polity that works through differences through the courts of the church.

The same issues were very much in play in the southern Presbyterian church in the 1960s and early 1970s when the Presbyterian Church in America (PCA) was founded. One could make the case, as I hope to do in a book tentatively titled *For a Continuing Church: Southern Presbyterians and Fundamentalism, 1934-74*, that the PCA was a fundamentalist group when it was created in 1973 and has spent the past thirty-five years trying to figure out what biblical Presbyterianism should be for the world today. How to transition from 'standing for truth' to 'loving the brothers' – or rather how to maintain this posture at the same time – is the continuing challenge for many of us today.

CHAPTER FOURTEEN

RAISING THE FOUNDATIONS

An Interview
with Gary L. W. Johnson

Gary L. W. Johnson is the Senior Minister of Church of the Redeemer, Mesa, Arizona. He has edited *B. B. Warfield: Essays on his life and thought* and co-edited, along with Ron Gleason, *Reforming or Conforming?*

MARTIN DOWNES: Have you ever been drawn toward any views or movements that time has shown to have been unhelpful or even dangerous?

GARY L. W. JOHNSON: Yes, and it happened in the last place I would have expected. I walked on to the campus of Westminster Theological Seminary in Philadelphia in 1978, just as the controversy swirling around Norman Shepherd was reaching a crescendo. Norman Shepherd, as you know, succeeded the acclaimed Scottish theologian John Murray (after his retirement in 1963) in the department of Systematic Theology. Around 1974, it became obvious that Shepherd's views on justification were starting to attract attention and alarm.

When I arrived, the campus was polarized. Shepherd had his faithful followers amongst the faculty and the student body, and I initially found myself drawn toward his views because of my own experience with the 'anti-Lordship' theology of Charles Ryrie, and those like him from Dallas Theological Seminary. This was traceable to my own background. I became a Christian shortly after I returned from serving in combat in Vietnam with the U.S. Army in 1971 and was nurtured in a 'Dallas' Bible church and the kind of things that were usually associated with those kind of churches, i.e. Hal Lindsey's books, Bill Bright and Campus Crusade for Christ.

DOWNES: How did you move away from this 'anti-Lordship' emphasis and toward Reformed theology?

JOHNSON: My exposure to the doctrines of grace, or Calvinism, as it is usually called, came through the tape ministry of the late S. Lewis Johnson, Jr. (who I later studied under and served as his teaching assistant at T.E.D.S. in 1983-84). It was Dr Johnson who introduced me to the Old Princeton men like Hodge, Warfield and Machen. He also directed me to Westminster.

DOWNES: Was the controversy at Westminster related to the difference between what has been pejoratively called 'easy believism' and Reformed theology?

JOHNSON: It appeared to me, and others at the time, that Shepherd's views were reactionary to the kind of teaching that characterized Evangelicalism as popularly expressed by Bill Bright and Campus Crusade for Christ, who were in turn deeply indebted to the kind of antinomian teaching that Ryrie and Zane Hodges gave scholarly credibility.

At first I understood Shepherd to be proposing an antidote to this kind of 'easy believism.' In fact Cornelius Van Til told us that he supported Shepherd because, 'Bill Bright is not right!' But, as the debate intensified, I began to see things differently.

DOWNES: How were Professor Shepherd's views perceived and responded to at Westminster during that time?

JOHNSON: In response to concerned faculty members, Shepherd prepared a discussion paper in 1976 of fifty-three pages, not intended for distribution, entitled, 'The Relation of Good Works to Justification in the Westminster Standards.' It made a startling and categorical statement: 'To insist on faith alone for justification is a serious impoverishment.'

He went on to claim that Westminster Standards supported his position much to the shock and consternation of a number of his fellow faculty members, Robert Strimple (Systematic Theology), Robert Godfrey (Church History), Meredith Kline (Old Testament), W. Stanford Reid (Church History), Philip Hughes (Reformation Studies), O. Palmer Robertson (Old Testament), and Robert Knudsen (Apologetics). I remember the open debates amongst various members of the faculty that were held in Van Til Hall. These were often very heated and animated!

Two of my classes quickly introduced me to the seriousness of this controversy. My course with W. Robert Godfrey, 'The Theology of The Counter Reformation', revealed that Shepherd had more in common with the Council of Trent than he did with the Reformers. (Godfrey, Reid and Hughes – all exceptional church historians – were accused by Shepherd of being 'Lutherans'. Needless to say they all found that charge absurd, but Shepherd and his disciples, in what goes by the label 'The Federal Vision', continue to make it – more about this later).

The other class, 'Old Testament Biblical Theology' with Meredith Kline, introduced me to the centrality of covenant theology, particularly the critical nature of the Covenant of Works in understanding the active and passive obedience of Christ in securing our salvation.

Shepherd admitted that a truly justified person could *lose* that justification, and as such (in his scheme) justification was subject to increase or decrease, something that his predecessor,

John Murray, emphatically denied in his gem of a book, *Redemption Accomplished and Applied.*

Among the more outspoken critics of Shepherd outside of the seminary community, included the late Martyn Lloyd-Jones, who called Shepherd's doctrine 'another gospel'. This is significant in light of John Frame's (who defended Shepherd then and now) recent inflammatory remarks in the *Backbone of The Bible* (ed. Andrew Sandlin), where he called Shepherd's critics 'stupid' and unfit to be theological teachers (a comment he later retracted). Frame, who was at WTS in Philadelphia during this period, knew about Lloyd-Jones' assessment, and that of other respected Reformed Theologians who likewise opposed Shepherd's views on justification.

In addition to Lloyd-Jones, these included Sinclair Ferguson, Roger Nicole, William Hendricksen and Gregg Singer (a good account of this situation is provided by A. Donald MacLeod's *W. Stanford Reid: An Evangelical Calvinist in the Academy*, published by McGill-Queen's University Press, 2004).

DOWNES: You mentioned Shepherd's comments that insisting on faith alone for justification was a 'serious impoverishment' and that perhaps his Reformed colleagues were really Lutheran in their views of justification. Was Luther's view warranted from Scripture?

JOHNSON: As I stated, Shepherd was very fond of accusing his Reformed opponents of being 'closet' Lutherans. As you know, *Allein durch den glauben*, is how Luther translated that key phrase in Romans 3:28 in his German Bible. His Roman Catholic opponents accused him of grossly perverting the Scripture by inserting the word allein (alone) into the text. Charles Hodge points out that Catholic translations, long before Luther, had rendered the passage the same way. The Nuremberg Bible of 1483 reads *Nur* (only) *durch den glauben* and even more surprising is that the Italian Bibles of Geneva (1476) and Venice (1538) read *per sola fide*. Luther responded to his critics by saying:

Note, then, whether Paul does not assert more vehemently that faith alone justifies than I do, although he does not use the word *alone (sola)*, which I have used. For he who says: Works do not justify, but faith justifies, certainly affirms more strongly that faith justifies than does he who says: Faith alone justifies...It is ridiculous enough to argue in this sophistical manner: Faith alone justifies; therefore the Holy Spirit does not justify. Or: The Spirit justifies; therefore not faith alone. For this is not what the dispute is about at this place. Rather the question is only about the relation of faith and works, whether anything is to be ascribed to works in justification. Since the apostle does not ascribe anything to them, he without doubt ascribes all to faith alone.

DOWNES: Did Calvin take a different view to Luther on justification by faith alone? Should we recognize a distinct Reformed view of justification by faith alone as opposed to a Lutheran view?

JOHNSON: Strange as it would appear, Luther's critics today include people who claim to be the true heirs of Calvin and the real representatives of the Reformed faith. Shepherd and Lusk both contend that a genuine Reformed understanding of justification is substantively different than Luther's. In fact, Shepherd and his disciple in the Federal Vision, Rich Lusk, are of the opinion that Luther's German translation of Romans 3:28 'actually distorts Paul's meaning.' Why? Because this would, in Shepherd's mind, 'cancel out the teaching of James,' (2:24) (cf. his article 'Justification by Faith Alone' in *Reformation and Revival Journal* [vol. 11, No. 2, Spring 2002]).

But Calvin agreed wholeheartedly with Luther. He wrote:

> Now the reader sees how fairly the Sophists today cavil against our doctrine when we say

that man is justified by faith alone [Rom. 3:28].
They dare not deny that man is justified by faith
because it recurs so often in Scripture. But since
the word 'alone' is nowhere expressed, they do
not allow this addition to be made. Is it so? But
what will they reply to these words of Paul where
he contends that righteousness cannot be of faith
unless it be free [Rom. 4:2ff.]? How will a free
gift agree with works? With what chicaneries
will they elude what he says in another passage,
that God's righteousness is revealed in the gospel
[Rom. 1:17]? If righteousness is revealed in the
gospel, surely no mutilated or half righteousness
but a full and perfect righteousness is contained
there. The law therefore has no place in it. Not
only by a false, but by an obviously ridiculous
shift, they insist upon excluding this adjective.
Does not he who takes everything from works
firmly enough ascribe everything to faith alone?
What, I pray, do these expressions mean; 'His
righteousness has been manifested apart from
the law' [Rom. 3:21]; and 'Man is freely justified'
[Rom. 3:24]; and 'Apart from the works of
the law' [Rom. 3:28]? *Institutes of the Christian
Religion* BK. III. Ch. 11, sec. 19.

DOWNES: Was this alleged radical disagreement between the
Lutheran and Reformed views of justification by faith alone
challenged at the time of the Shepherd controversy?

JOHNSON: W. Stanford Reid was well aware of Shepherd's
efforts to divide the two reformers. As one of the most
respected church historians of the twentieth century, Reid
marshaled an impressive testimony from Calvin's own
writings to counter Shepherd's claims. He observed that the
position Shepherd was advancing did have historical roots

– but it is Richard Baxter, and not the Reformers (especially Calvin), who mirrors Shepherd's views. Reid observed:

> Richard Baxter and others even came to be known as 'new-nomians' because of their stress upon good works, as though they were an aid in obtaining justification. And this attitude has continued in some circles even to our own day, when some Reformed theologians could term the doctrine of justification by faith alone as 'easy believism' and insist that such a doctrine is Lutheran rather than Reformed.
>
> For these reasons it would seem to be a good thing to look back to one who is recognized as the theologian who largely formulated the basic Reformed doctrines in the sixteenth century. Moreover, that he was a contemporary of Martin Luther and knew exactly what Luther was teaching helps us to understand whether or not he was in favor of Luther's formulation of the doctrine of justification by faith. If he disagreed, he would certainly have said so, while on the other hand, if he agreed there would also be a clear indication of this fact…Calvin was not hesitant to lay great stress upon the doctrine of 'justification by faith alone.'
>
> While he admits that the qualifying term is never employed specifically in the Bible, he insists that the concept or idea is implicit in such passages as Romans 4:22ff; 1:17; 3:21 and Galatians 3:10ff. The editor of the most recent English edition of the Institutes points out in a footnote how often in 3:17:7, 8, 10 the term 'faith alone' is repeated. God is propitious to us as soon as we by faith rest 'on the blood of Christ,' a phrase which he explains to mean the 'whole

work of expiation.' Thus since faith alone is the means by which one receives justification and reconciliation to God, the merit of every work 'falls to the ground.' Therefore, if justification by faith alone is a specifically Lutheran doctrine, we must put Calvin in the Lutheran rather than in the Reformed camp.' W. Stanford Reid, 'Justification By Faith According to John Calvin.' *The Westminster Theological Journal* (Vol. XLII. No. 2, Spring 1980).

DOWNES: After professor Shepherd left Westminster Seminary, Philadelphia, did the controversy die down?

JOHNSON: After Shepherd was dismissed from WTS (and fled the OPC for the CRC when it became evident that charges would be brought against him in his presbytery) it appeared that his novel views would no longer trouble the Reformed churches, and for almost twenty years this was the case. But things changed in 2000 when Shepherd published a little book entitled *The Call of Grace: How The Covenant Illuminates Salvation and Evangelism* (P & R). Shepherd was back and as it turned out, he had a sizeable following.

John Armstrong, for one, began to aggressively promote Shepherd, first in the pages of his *Reformation and Revival Journal* (which he later renamed *ACT III*), and then in his conferences (the latest is scheduled for this coming Fall). But perhaps even more significant is the group known as 'The Federal Vision'. The Federal Vision, which was birthed at the Auburn Avenue Presbyterian Church (PCA) in Monroe, LA. in 2002, originally had scheduled Shepherd to be the keynote speaker at its pastors' conference in 2002 (due to personal issues, Shepherd could not come, and he was replaced by one of his disciples, John Barach).

DOWNES: How has Shepherd's understanding of the Reformed view of justification been articulated in the Federal Vision?

JOHNSON: Running through the 'new and improved' proposals on justification being offered by the advocates of The New Perspective on Paul and the followers of Norman Shepherd in the Federal Vision is an insipid form of what I call *sola bootstrapa*, i.e., in some aspect our final justification is ultimately traced to our own efforts to maintain 'covenantal faithfulness'.

If words mean anything, then we are forced to read these kinds of statements at face value. Here are two in particular. This is how new perspective sympathizer Don Garlington (who as it turns out is also a product of Westminster Seminary in Philadelphia) puts it in commenting on Romans 8:1: 'not withstanding our many failures, there is no condemnation *as long as we desire* to remain within the covenant bond, true to Christ the Lord' (italics mine).

Or again, these words from Rich Lusk of the Federal Vision: 'Initial reception of the white garment is by faith alone; ongoing possession of the garment is maintained by faithful obedience ... Their 'whiteness' before the Father's throne is due solely to His death and resurrection. In this sense, the robes stand for initial justification. But this forensic justification cannot be separated from the *good works* that *make the saints worthy of their new apparel*. In other words, the poetic imagery points in the same direction as the theological prose of Paul (Rom. 2:13 and James 2:14ff): those who will be vindicated in the end are those who have been faithfully obedient.'

Again, if words mean anything then, we are forced to read them at face value, and only the most devoted defenders of the Federal Vision will not see this statement of Lusk as an explicit denial of *sola fide*. Although all of these men (who insist they are 'Reformed') would vigorously protest the charge, in the final analysis they claim that our justification is the result of the grace of God in Christ *plus* our own efforts to stay in a state of justification by maintaining covenantal faithfulness.

DOWNES: Does this not jeopardize the Reformation doctrines of *sola fide* and *sola gratia*?

JOHNSON: Our mutual friend, Scott Clark of Westminster Seminary in California, underscored this recently by pointing out 'To say "*and cooperation with grace*" is to change the formula completely because it attempts to synthesize two contrary principles: grace and works. When it comes to justification there is no synthesizing grace and works. Either we stand before the perfectly holy God on the basis of the perfect righteousness of Christ imputed to us sinners and received by grace alone, or we do not. It is not possible to say 'by grace *and* works.' If it is by grace, then it is not by works, and if it is in the tiniest bit by our works, i.e., our cooperation with grace, then it is not by grace. This is what Paul says in Romans 11:6, 'But if it is by grace, it is no longer on the basis of works; otherwise grace would no longer be grace' or in 2 Timothy 1:9, 'in Christ Jesus before the ages began.'

DOWNES: It seems strange that those who identify themselves as Reformed should advance an interpretation of justification that undermines the historic Reformed view. How do you account for this?

JOHNSON: Millard Erickson, an esteemed Evangelical theologian recently made this observation:

> We often interpret a bit of data, even a differing view, through our own unconscious assumptions. Frequently we even state the terms of the discussion from our own perspective. To fail to realize that this is how we see it because of our presuppositions is to doom us to confusion and erroneous interpretation from the very beginning. Most of us are much better at identifying others' presuppositions and the influence of those upon their thought than at recognizing and acknowledging the same about ourselves.

Are the representatives of these new proposals self-consciously advancing a form of semi-pelagianism? Probably not – but it is there. The overt semi-pelagianism at work in these new proposals has not gone unnoticed.

Richard Gaffin, one of my former professors at Westminster Theological Seminary, pointed this out when he wrote in reference to two of the most significant representatives of the New Perspective on Paul, J. D. G. Dunn and N. T. Wright:

> When I consider the conclusions that our two authors reach on Paul's understanding of sin, I cannot help but envision the tired but knowing smile of Princeton theologian Charles Hodge, observing, as he surveys the ebb and flow of Church history, that it's not so much the ghost of Pelagius that he fears as the ghost of semi-Pelagius!? As in the case of most cases of semi-pelagianism, there is a failure to fully comprehend the dire condition of our fallenness and existing wretchedness.

It should be pointed out that Gaffin was early on, one of Shepherd's defenders, but as Shepherd continued on his trajectory that now includes the open rejection of the Covenant of Works and the imputation of the active obedience of Christ, as well as his confusing definition of what constitutes 'saving' faith, Gaffin (as his role in the OPC study report demonstrates) no longer supports Shepherd.

DOWNES: Where does all this place the views of Shepherd, the Federal Vision authors you referred to, and others who are recasting justification for today?

JOHNSON: I am forced to conclude that judged by our Reformed Confession, Norman Shepherd, N.T. Wright and their disciples like John Armstrong, and especially some of the advocates of the Federal Vision, despite their loud claim to the contrary, are *not* Reformed. The Federal Vision is plagued by anti-Reformed distinctives, i.e., all baptized people are actually saved until they fall away. A person is considered *elect* by virtue of their union with Christ in baptism, but can become *non-elect* through covenantal unfaithfulness. The forgiveness of sins, which is an essential part of justification can be forfeited. All of this is contrary to the Westminster Standards, and I will not grant them the right to call themselves Calvinists (nor do I think Calvin would be pleased by this crowd claiming to be his disciples!).

CHAPTER FIFTEEN

TEACHING THE WHOLE COUNSEL OF GOD

An Interview with Conrad Mbewe

Conrad Mbewe is Pastor of Kabwata Baptist Church, Lusaka, Zambia.

MARTIN DOWNES: What are the most common theological errors that you have to deal with as a pastor?

CONRAD MBEWE: The most common theological errors that I have had to deal with as a pastor are at three levels. The first has to do with the way of salvation, the second has to do with the work of the Holy Spirit, and the third has to do with the nature of spiritual success.

With respect to the way of salvation, the main error is that all forms of 'works' have been introduced to replace grace through faith alone. Roman Catholicism is rife in Zambia. Hence their error that good works play a part in salvation is equally common in the land. Then, we also have the modern Charismatic movement that has an extreme form of Arminianism in its understanding of the way of salvation. They will assure anyone who walks to the front after an altar call and repeats a sinner's prayer that they are saved. With so many crusades being conducted all over Zambia, we meet a lot of people who have gone through this factory-line and have been assured that they are now Christians but who fail every biblical test of salvation.

With respect to the work of the Holy Spirit, the main error is found in the Charismatic movement which has grown by leaps and bounds in the recent past. Ultimately they see Him as a power that you can summon to your aid if you pray long enough and loud enough. Listening to most of their preachers, one gets the impression that the Holy Spirit responds to formulas – and they have the right formula.

Coupled with this preoccupation with the Holy Spirit, there is a growing preoccupation with the devil. At one time it was usually only found in sermons and in prayers, as they would be binding Satan over and over again. Now there is a growing suspicion of Satanism. Anyone who is progressing and is not in their circles must be a Satanist! It has become a Christian form of witch-hunting. Sadly, this is the centre of so much Christian talk, instead of the Lord Jesus.

With respect to the nature of spiritual success, the main error is what has been coined as 'the health and wealth gospel'. Again, this is largely from the growing Charismatic movement. This error has given worldliness legitimacy in the Christian church. Humility, sacrifice and generosity are becoming rare virtues. Christians with weak frames are finding very little to identify with in the churches. There are many casualties from this spiritual environment. Yet the error continues to be propagated because it is what the crowds with itching ears want to hear.

DOWNES: How do you put into practice personally and among the elders in your church Paul's admonition to keep watch on yourselves (Acts 20:30-31)?

MBEWE: There are a number of spiritual activities we engage in as elders to help one another in this self-watch. The first is that we have a comprehensive oversight visitation program that includes the homes of the elders. In this program, we visit the homes of all the church members with a view to ascertain how they are doing and help them with some of the issues they are wrestling with. Elders' homes are included in this visitation. Secondly, we have fortnightly elders' prayer meetings.

In between these meetings, we read the same books and then share the insights we are getting from these books. In this way, we are learning together and sharpening one another in practical and doctrinal subjects. Finally, we maintain very open relationships, where we are free to deal with one another honestly following the channels set forth by the Lord in Matthew 18.

If any elder feels rather concerned about any other elder, he must visit him alone and seek to deal with the matter of concern that he has observed. Where this is not reaping any desired fruit, he is to go with another elder in an informal capacity. If even this does not bear any fruit, then the two are obligated to bring the matter up officially at the next elders' meeting so that the brother is confronted in that forum. In this way we keep watch on ourselves.

DOWNES: How have you dealt with church members who have been attracted or taken in by false teaching?

MBEWE: My answer to this question may surprise you, but in the twenty years I have been a pastor of my church, I have not dealt with church members who have imbibed any of the false teachings I have mentioned above. I think that it is because from the very beginning I have maintained a doctrinal emphasis in my preaching, whether the sermons are evangelistic or meant for the edification of believers. By stating from the very beginning of my pastoral ministry that I am a Reformed Baptist, and moving the church to the point where it has adopted the *1689 Baptist Confession of Faith*, I think that individuals join our church knowing very well what we believe and seeking to know what it means to be 'Reformed'.

Every second year of my pastorate, I have held seminars in which I have dealt with the main doctrinal issues that the church needed to work through in order to be clear as to what the Bible taught concerning those issues. The materials presented in these seminars have subsequently been printed in booklet form and kept on the market so that those joining the church later are able to just purchase them (or download them freely from the church website) and catch up on these matters.

I also think that because my pulpit ministry is of a consecutive expository fashion, church members have learned to see the truth in its biblical context. Hence they are able to discern when someone is using texts out of context in order to peddle their own teachings. So, I have not had any experience in dealing with church members holding on to serious error.

DOWNES: Calvin said that ministers have two voices. One is for the sheep and the other for warding off the wolves. How have you struck the right balance in this regard in your pulpit ministry?

MBEWE: As stated under that last question, the church is in no doubt what I believe because I have stated it. The church itself has a doctrinal basis that is detailed enough for them to know what they ought to believe as members. And I maintain a consecutive expository preaching ministry that develops believers in their own Bible study approach. In this way, the church is preserved from doctrinal error by being pointed again and again to the truth as it is found in its biblical context.

In my preaching ministry, I do not hesitate to state errors that are in direct conflict with truth that is evident in the text. What I rarely do is mention names of individuals who are teaching that error. I think that by handling the truth primarily and in the secondary sense mention the errors that are in conflict with these truths, I have struck the right balance in my pulpit ministry.

DOWNES: How should a pastor protect the flock and help them to value sound doctrine when he knows that they could well be influenced by an overload of unhelpful teaching from books, conferences, television, and the internet?

MBEWE: I definitely do not think that we should be too protective, as though we alone are immune to error and our people are not. By that I mean that we cannot ban them from reading certain books, attending certain conferences, watching certain TV channels or visiting certain internet sites. That would be going against liberty of conscience. As I said earlier, our main role is that of teaching the truth in its biblical context and our people will be able to discern error. There will be a stability in their lives that will keep them away from seeking that which looks like bread at a distance but is actually a stone!

DOWNES: Are there any doctrines that you think are being neglected in preaching today?

MBEWE: This is a very difficult question to answer because I do not think that as pastors we should be preaching doctrines. I think that as pastors we should be preaching in a consecutive expository fashion. Our main aim should not be to preach all the doctrines but the whole of the Bible. By that I do not mean every verse of the Bible, but that we balance our preaching so that our sermons cover the Old and the New Testament, the Gospels and the Epistles, the historical and poetic passages, etc.

May I add that we are to also maintain a balance between evangelistic preaching and that which is for the edification of the saints. While we are doing that, our people should see how consistent the Bible is doctrinally and in the end they will develop a systematic theology in their minds without even realizing it. This will help them to fill in the dotted lines when handling doctrines that we have not touched ourselves.

Preaching in a consecutive expository fashion helps us to keep the balance of truth that the Holy Spirit Himself has put in the Scriptures. We will be prevented from riding our own hobby horse each time we are in the pulpit. This is what will keep us also from neglecting any important doctrines. I have no doubt that if there are any doctrines being neglected today it is because preachers are not preaching through the Scriptures in a consecutive expository fashion.

DOWNES: What is the best way for a busy pastor to keep informed of contemporary theological issues when he knows that there is simply not enough time to read all the books? Could you name a handful of critical issues and the best material on them?

MBEWE: I am in Africa and so some of the critical issues I have to contend with may be totally irrelevant to your readers in the West. I have named a few already in answer to your first question. For instance, there is a real need for pastors to be clear about the gospel. If we lose the gospel, we have lost our very right to stand in the pulpit. There are too many false gospels doing their rounds and every pastor must be aware that his 'gospel' is not one of them.

Similarly, being in Africa also means that it is not just the time that I do not have in order to read all the books. The pocket also cannot allow me the luxury of buying all the books that I may want! I find that the best answer to this problem is to subscribe to a good journal or two. I find that journals like the *Banner of Truth* magazine and *Reformation Today* magazine tend to be brief, easy reading and contemporary enough for me to be forewarned about the critical issues in the theological world today. In their reference lists, I also see the books that I ought to be on the lookout for if I want to do further reading on those critical issues. I suppose that my limited scope is primarily due to the place where I ply out my trade. Your readers will probably have such a wide variety of journals that they may know of some which are far better than those that I have just mentioned. My answer to the question of the best materials to read in a busy pastorate is still, 'Subscribe to a few good journals.'

DOWNES: The New Testament warns us about the subtlety of error. If false teaching isn't always obvious what principles should we apply so that we keep ourselves from being deceived?

MBEWE: I think that the number one principle in seeing through the subtlety of error is learning to handle truth in its biblical context. As someone has said, 'A text without a context is a pretext' – it is a lie! It is often pretty clear to any discerning mind when a text has been wrested out of its comfortable context in order to say what someone else wants it to say. When I listen to many preachers today and they state something which makes my hair stand on end, I will often wait for them to prove it from the Bible. I often find that all I need to do is dig around the verses they would have quoted and I find that there has been a gross misapplication of Scripture. The Holy Spirit was saying one thing when He inspired the sacred writer, and the preacher is saying something totally different.

Where the context is not able to help, the second principle is that obscure passages of the Bible must be interpreted by those passages of the Bible that are more perspicuous. In other words, Scripture does not contradict itself since its primary author is the same Holy Spirit. So, if a false teacher quotes Scripture to suit his situation but it contradicts the clear teaching of another passage of the Bible, it should send all the warning signals that you are in danger and ought to tread carefully. Is that not how the Lord Jesus handled Satan when he tempted Him using the Scriptures in Matthew 4? Jesus simply referred to other Scriptures that were clearly being violated by the meaning that Satan was putting upon the Scriptures he was quoting. We should do the same!

DOWNES: Why does God allow His church to be troubled by false teachers?

MBEWE: It is simply because the church is still in the world! I cannot see it any other way. Jesus gave a parable about the nature of the kingdom of God (Matt. 13:24-30). He talked about a farmer sowing wheat in his field and at night an enemy came and sowed tares. The wheat and the tares are to grow together until harvest time. Clearly, He was teaching that while God is busy with the work of the salvation of sinners and the sanctification of saints in His church, Satan will also be busy confusing all this by planting his own false teachers in the church, and that it will be so for the rest of history until He (the Lord Jesus) returns. That is when He will separate the two permanently.

It is the very nature of sin that it is first of all wrong belief. That is how sin entered into human life. Satan, through the subtlety of the serpent, brought doubt into Eve's mind about God's instructions and God's pure motives. Once Eve's mind was polluted with this wrong belief, she was a sitting duck for him! So, it is not so much that God is allowing His church to be troubled by false teachers as simply the fact that God has not shielded His church from the world of sin. Sin is in our hearts and in the world around us, and so let us not be surprised that it is in the church also. Just as we are seeking to root it out through the truth of the Word in our hearts and in the world, so also must we let the light of the Word beam on its darkness even in the church. However, just as sin will never be totally uprooted until the Lord returns, so also its vanguard – error – will remain with us until then.

DOWNES: There are so many errors facing evangelicals today it would be easy to become preoccupied with them (and we would all love to think that wasn't the case). So how can we take error seriously, be rightly informed about it, but not be so taken up with it that our lives become distorted?

MBEWE: Again, I go back to consecutive expository preaching. Let us simply teach the Word of God regularly, in its own context, and we shall find that we will not be preoccupied with error. We will be overwhelmed with the grandeur and beauty of the truth, as set forth in the Scriptures, that we will be lost in wonder, love and praise to God for this truth instead of starting at anything that moves, for fear that it may be erroneous. We will also have a passion for the truth without necessarily being trigger-happy and sniffing out error under every bush and shrub. So, I repeat my appeal for consecutive expository preaching. That is the answer, the biblical answer to avoid our lives as Christians becoming distorted.

DOWNES: Is there a point of no return for those who embrace heresies?

MBEWE: No one is beyond redemption while he still has breath in him. Humanly speaking, there are some individuals who have so immersed themselves in error that we look at them with a sense of hopelessness. Some of them have even made themselves apostles of error. They are crusaders for their brand of heresy. Where can one start from to disentangle them from their labyrinth of error? One can only despair!

However, the words of Martin Luther should bring hope to our hearts:

> And though this world, with devils filled,
> Should threat to undo us,
> We will not fear, for God hath willed
> His truth to triumph through us.
> The prince of darkness grim,
> We tremble not for him;
> His rage we can endure,
> For lo! his doom is sure;
> One little word shall fell him.

Let us continue to preach the truth in its biblical context. Those who are God's true children will hear the voice of their Shepherd and follow Him. However entangled they may be in the shrubs of deceit, the voice of the Shepherd will ring true in their hearts and they shall follow Him until they lie in green pastures beside quiet waters. Amen and amen!

CHAPTER SIXTEEN

PRESENT ISSUES FROM A LONG TERM PERSPECTIVE

*An Interview
with Geoffrey Thomas*

For over forty years Geoff Thomas has been Pastor of Alfred Place Baptist Church, Aberystwyth, West Wales. He is the author of *The Sure Word of God* and *Daniel: Servant of God under four kings*.

MARTIN DOWNES: As you reflect back to your days in seminary and early years in the ministry were there men who started out with evangelical convictions who later moved away from the gospel? How did you cope with that?

GEOFFREY THOMAS: In a groaning fallen world there have to be those who initially receive the word with joy and then the cares of the world and the deceitfulness of wealth and position draw them away into apostasy. Our Savior warned us about that. There are indeed fellow seminarians who have rejected the faith, and we have nothing to do with one another these days. Of course they live on the opposite side of the Atlantic.

My chief response is to wonder what part I had to play in that departure. In other words, I was superficial, carnal, light and worldly when they needed as companions students who were filled with the fragrance of Christ, tender, prayerful, gracious. If I had been like that to them while we studied together that is bound to have helped them when the roaring lion sought to devour them. I let them down. Yet Ryle and Wilberforce lived a consistent godly life and their sons rejected their fathers' faith, and so one cannot whip oneself with the thought that it was exclusively one's own inconsistencies that caused these falls. There were others of us who talked the talk but failed to walk the walk.

Downes: Have you ever been drawn toward any views or movements that time has shown to have been unhelpful or even dangerous theologically?

Thomas: Yes. It happened to me at Westminster Seminary under the influence of the late Dr Ed Palmer, taking the apologetics of Van Til into areas where Van Til himself was wise and godly enough not to enter. I gained a lop-sided emphasis on culture and social involvement and that led to the externalization of the doctrines of grace, especially justification and regeneration. Hitherto they had been for me enfleshed in the ministries of Whitefield and Spurgeon but then the world and life view swamped them.

I was intoxicated by engagement with the world and my criticisms of 'pietism' were really a restlessness with the stringent demands of biblical piety. It was a barren world which I dallied with while at the same time getting my inspiration from Puritanism. I tried to hold onto both but found it impossible. My preaching of justification was an offer to sinners of an inner occurrence wherein the living Word in union with the Spirit introduces whoever trusts the Lord Jesus into the spiritual reality of Christ and His realm.

A zeal for the kingship of Christ in the world led to an acceleration of the process of the secularization of spiritual values. The biblical faith became more and more externalized or hollowed out. Fellow students were contaminated by the spirit of the age. The doctrine of common grace had become more enchanting than redeeming grace. The individual heart and soul was neglected and an emphasis on its needs dismissed as 'individualism'!

DOWNES: How should a minister keep his heart, mind and will from theological error?

THOMAS: God keeps us from falling. He can send barrenness into our lives when we wander away, and anyone who has tasted and seen that the Lord is good cries with Newton, 'How tedious and tasteless the hours when Jesus no longer I see.' He revives our souls; He gives us a taste for warm fellowship, lively preaching, books that make the truth spirit and life.

How important to read Calvin, Brooks, Watson, Bunyan, Whitefield's diary, Spurgeon, M'Cheyne, the Bonars, Edwards, Ryle, Whyte, Machen, Lloyd-Jones, Iain Murray's writings, John Murray, Packer and Motyer. How important to find some preachers whose sermons are a blessing to our souls. I go to as many conferences as I can where experiential biblical Christianity is promoted. I read the magazines that support that perspective. I meet each month with a fraternal of ten men who love those truths. I meet each Friday morning at 7 a.m. to pray for a revival of God's truth in our day. I preach three times a week from Old and New Testaments, always looking for new ground to break.

DOWNES: Calvin said that ministers have two voices. One is for the sheep and the other for warding off the wolves. How have you struck the right balance in this regard in your pulpit ministry?

THOMAS: For every single word addressed to the wolf give ten words to the sheep. These are very uncomfortable days for Christians and God's great Word to His shepherds is 'Comfort ye my people.' There are proportionately in the Bible, as well as gospel promises, warning notes which in the course of one's ministry one must sound. They are not as soul-satisfying as words that address the sheep.

For example, I have preached from the text, 'I urge you, brothers, to watch out for those who cause divisions and put obstacles in your way that are contrary to the teaching you have learned. Keep away from them. For such people are not serving our Lord Christ, but their own appetites. By smooth talk and flattery they deceive the minds of naïve people' (Rom. 16:17, 18). My task is to preach that passage knowing that such men are at our door threatening our souls.

I will preach those warnings as serving Him who in the Sermon on the Mount warned of false prophets and wolves in sheep's clothing. The best protector of sheep is a vigilant loving Shepherd. A fit sheep can run to Him when it sees a wolf coming while a sickly starving sheep has no energy to try to escape from one who desires its death. Make the sheep as healthy as they can be.

DOWNES: Good men can end up with an excessively negative ministry when they become preoccupied with error. This of course was a point made by Dr Martyn Lloyd-Jones in his conversation with T. T. Shields. How can a minister keep himself from this temptation?

THOMAS: I didn't enjoy reading that encounter given from Lloyd-Jones' angle exclusively, nor those other memories of his conversations with men he differs with, when he comes off the best. I think that in that glorious book of his, *Preaching and Preachers*, they are the weakest elements. There was an awful American fundamentalism which announced sermons on 'The five greatest sinners in town', etc, but Shields was far from that. He was a giant. Lloyd-Jones himself was very concerned with error in Anglican leadership, and Billy Graham, and institutions in America and Scotland.

One thing I loved about the staff at Westminster Seminary was when men claiming to be evangelical in their beliefs wrote erroneously and then their books were reviewed and their errors were spelled out by Van Til, John Murray, E.J.Young and Meredith Kline. The book reviews and articles of the

Westminster Theological Journal were read as a benchmark for all of us forty to fifty years ago. C. S. Lewis, treated as a prophet by American Christianity, was not spared, nor even was Francis Schaeffer. That engagement with popular religion has totally gone and I am weaker as a result. One has to look elsewhere for an analysis of Christian hedonism, seeker-friendly worship services, new covenant theology, anti-nomianism, the federal vision, the purpose-driven church and life.

Downes: How have you dealt with church members or students who have been attracted or taken in by false teaching?

Thomas: Not always very well. I have not familiarized myself with it or been able to answer it as biblically as I should. The congregation's loyalty to me as a person has won the day for me more than their persuasion that I was answering the errorist.

There are 67 varieties of error in the professing church. I am not going to tell a congregation of the Graf-Wellhausen theory and then point out its errors. They will not come across it, but a student in the final years in school or at the university taking some biblical studies course will meet it. I will brush up my O. T. Allis's *The Five Books of Moses* (which today is still unanswerable because it is so thorough) and loan it to him to read. New error is provocative and it takes a time to understand.

For the last few years people have come to me and said, 'What exactly is the New Perspective on the Apostle Paul?' How difficult it has been to answer them. I can answer now better than three years ago, but that debate is for the mandarins, and increasingly the paedo-baptist mandarins, not the people I preach to who need to understand and glory in the free justification of the New Testament.

Downes: I have heard it said that in their theology and practice older ministers can either become too soft and indulgent, or that they can become too hard and pessimistic. How are you handling this issue?

THOMAS: Someone recently asked me was it true that I had got softer in my old age? I don't remember if his word was 'softer' but that was the impression I got. I am not sure. I still believe that Machen's *Christianity and Liberalism* is the truest analysis of the religion that took over in Wales in the twentieth century and destroyed the impact of the church on the nation causing the salt to lose its savior.

Modernism is another religion, not Christianity even though it uses God's words. I refuse to participate in any ecumenical activities, any weeks of prayer for Christian unity – let them pray to get Christian truth!

I still believe that the charismatic movement is a grand delusion. Anyone who claims he has the gift of miracles and healing is a crook and liar. Tongues speaking is gibberish and I seek to wean students from it by getting them to repeat aloud psalms in their quiet times rather than relax into tongues.

I believe in baptisms or fillings of the Spirit in giving men glorious power to preach the word – like that sermon of Al Martin on John 3, preached at the EMW conference at Aberystwyth in August 1970, but I do not believe that there are two classes of Christians, Spirit-baptized and non-Spirit-baptized. You cannot find that anywhere in the Bible. Men are given a special endowment of God, like the Lord Jesus was, for public ministry. There are wonderful experiences of God in preaching and in listening to preaching. People weep.

Am I becoming too indulgent or too hard? If the line between error and truth is a razor's edge and not a chasm then it is certainly true of this division. I firmly believe that in many cases it is the duty of the preacher to marry a Christian to a non-Christian, after a rebuke has been publicly administered. I think it wrong to throw them and their families and friends out of a church or get oneself ejected from the church over an issue like this. Counsel them. Marry them. Counsel and evangelize them again, but don't discard them. That may be a mark of my being soft in the head.

DOWNES: What would you consider to be the main theological dangers confronting us today and how can we deal with them?

THOMAS: The dumbing down of worship; the manufacture of 'Coca Cola lite' through the introduction of the band with its drums and insistent rhythm, the exclusive use of contemporary worship music as in the little university Christian Unions, the women reading and leading the service, the importance of humor for gauging the blessing of God in the participation of the congregation – that they laughed and enjoyed themselves, and preaching being a huge chunk of Scripture explained with Powerpoint like a glorified Bible Study. Help!

Where is the sorrow of heart for sin, breathings after God, hatred of self, living desires towards the Lord of life and glory, separation of spirit from the things of time and sense, faith in exercise, hope casting forth its anchor, love drawing forth the affections. What health; not in the feelings of excitement and rhythm and laughter but occasions when you really hate yourself, and feel what a base wretch you are and sigh after the Lord to come down and visit my soul, when you feel a little spirituality of mind, and taste a sweetness in the word of God and thank God again for sending to you such a Savior.

My soul is sick when sin reigns and rules; it is healthy when grace more or less predominates. Our worship and preaching must reflect that, tracing out the workings of grace in and under corruptions. Spiritual life is struggling against death, godly fear leading to self-abhorrence, groans and sighs under a guilty conscience, cries for deliverance, pantings after God, and so on - these are marks of life

There is a precious experience, and there is a vile experience, and the spokesman of God must encourage both in the sinner and the saint. I find the experience of the Scriptures that of mourning, complaint, sorrow of heart, pantings after God, hoping and trusting in His mercy and delightful assurance of faith.

DOWNES: It is natural that a younger generation can find it harder to navigate the theological currents in the church. With all your ministerial experience what advice would you give to younger ministers as they assess and handle various movements today?

THOMAS: Gain as many good role models as you can. If you depart from the confessions of faith then find the strongest arguments why our fathers resisted the path you are taking and seek to answer them. Wait until you are forty before coming down on the side of a position different from historical confessional Christianity (and wait until you are fifty before you use powerpoint!).

You think at twenty-four you can make safe judgments on the Spirit, and the law, and baptism, and evangelistic methods. I doubt it. Keep the narrow path until you are forty. You have all the New Testament church had – the means of grace, the Word of God, prayer, godly living. It is enough for these to master you without going out on a limb in a display of innovation, which spirit cannot keep you in a church for a lifetime.

Don't worry about getting one particular version of the Bible. There are half a dozen which are trustworthy and serious which you can use to bring the whole counsel of God to a congregation. There are two or three hymnbooks with another on its way which can satisfy any congregation and provide 400 hymns, so that you need not repeat a hymn in a year. Do not fight over those issues. Our war is with the world not with fellow believers whom we are pastoring and leading.

Personal prayer and the devotional life is still the most challenging and neglected part of our own ministries, and my deepest regret.

Chapter Seventeen

MINISTRY AMONG SHEEP AND WOLVES

An Interview
with Joel Beeke

Dr Joel Beeke serves as Pastor of the Heritage Netherlands Reformed Congregation, Grand Rapids, Michigan and is President and Professor of systematic theology at Puritan Reformed Theological Seminary. He is the author of numerous books including *The Quest for Full Assurance* and *Meet the Puritans*.

MARTIN DOWNES: As you reflect back to your days in seminary and early years in the ministry, were there men who started out with evangelical convictions who later moved away from the gospel? How did you cope with that?

JOEL BEEKE: I can only think of a few men with whom I had some personal acquaintance who have fallen from evangelical convictions. Initially, these rare situations shook me – particularly one Reformed brother with whom I studied at Westminster Seminary who embraced Roman Catholicism. Praying for their awakening and return, and for myself that I might not stumble nor look down haughtily upon them, has helped me cope. Then, I suppose, so have the daily challenges of the ministry which press me to keep my hand on the plow and not become overly distracted by an erring brother or two.

I know far more ministerial colleagues – numbering well into the hundreds – who have moved from non-evangelical positions to a solid evangelical and Reformed stance. Many of them suffered greatly, losing large portions, if not all, of their congregations in the process. I have often been profoundly encouraged by their courageous stance to contend earnestly for the faith which was once delivered unto the saints (Jude 3).

DOWNES: Have you ever been drawn toward any views or movements that time has shown to have been unhelpful or even dangerous theologically?

BEEKE: By the grace of God, no.

DOWNES: How should a minister keep his own heart, mind and will from theological error?

BEEKE: Keep yourself deeply immersed in the Scriptures, and pray daily to be willing to surrender all to their inerrant truth. Surround yourself with sound, godly colleagues and lay people who love you sufficiently to be honest with you, so that iron will sharpen iron.

Read the best, sound, scriptural, classic books, especially those by the Reformers and Puritans, that address your mind with clarity, convict your conscience with poignancy, bend your will with conviction, and move your feet with passion.

Meditate on those truths preached that do your people the most good; in every case, you will discover that they are biblical truths. Develop the hide of a rhinoceros so that you won't be tossed about with every criticism and wind of doctrine while maintaining the heart of a child, so that you will be a tender undershepherd to the needy.

DOWNES: Calvin said that ministers have two voices. One is for the sheep and the other for warding off the wolves. How have you struck the right balance in this regard in your pulpit ministry?

BEEKE: I suppose that one can never be absolutely certain that he is striking the right balance on this critical subject, but here are four guidelines that I find helpful:

1. Pray daily for biblical balance in all areas of ministry.
2. Love your sheep. Love has a way of balancing out our often imbalanced personalities. Those in error can receive much more from a minister who obviously loves them than from one who comes across as combative.
3. Be patient with your sheep. Be willing to teach them the same truth repeatedly, just as the Lord has done with you (cf. Phil. 3:1; 2 Pet. 3:1–2).
4. Let your 'voice for the sheep' always receive the primary accent of your ministry. Truth must ultimately be positive in nature to win the day with a congregation. Many ministers have focused too much on polemical and apologetical theology, often setting up and beating upon straw men in their congregation to the detriment of the flock. Polemics and apologetics must have the proper place of a minor accent in the ministry, so that no error is left unexposed.

But the minister must expose error wisely, forthrightly, humbly, compellingly, not by lording it over the sheep (2 Tim. 4:1–2; 1 Pet. 5:2–3).

DOWNES: Why do old heresies persist today? Why do men possessed of fine intellectual gifts end up embracing and believing significant theological errors?

BEEKE: Heresy is the product of the mind of 'the natural man', as Paul puts it in 1 Corinthians 2:14, that is, 'the unrenewed man' (Charles Hodge), who must necessarily receive and understand Christian truth without the illumination of the Holy Spirit and without a renewed mind. As a stranger to 'the wisdom of God' revealed in the gospel, he must also consult and depend on 'the wisdom of this world' (1 Cor. 1:19–24). Compounding the problem is the vanity of his mind, his darkened understanding, his ignorance and blindness of heart (Eph. 4:17–18). Such a man can have at best only a shallow, imperfect, distorted view of the truth, and it is not surprising that he conceives and propagates a multitude of errors and falsehoods.

The root of our English word 'heresy' is the Greek word *hairesis,* meaning 'choice' or 'opinion'. Note that the word implies the activity of both the mind and the will of man. Having come to a misunderstanding of the truth or having concocted or embraced a falsehood in its place, the natural man cleaves to his errors and zealously asserts and advances them precisely because they are his own opinions.

Nor is it surprising that when a false prophet or teacher begins to proclaim his erroneous views to others, there are many willing to receive and embrace them. Fallen men are hostile to the truth of God and prefer to believe a falsehood rather than submit to that truth. The wonder is not that there are many heretics, but that there are not many, many more.

Because the mind of the natural man is finite, there are only so many erroneous or heretical views it can conceive or embrace. Because that mind is corrupt and the corruption is inherited by succeeding generations, there is a tendency to resurrect or reproduce the errors of the past. After 2000 years, it is only to be expected that the errors and heresies of the present day all seem to have their historical antecedents, often reaching back to the earliest history and experience of the ancient church.

Ignorance always serves the cause of error. Christians who do not know what the Bible says and have no knowledge of the history of Christian doctrine find themselves unequipped to detect and refute these resurrected errors and heresies of the past. As a result, it is all too easy for false teachers 'to creep in unawares' (Jude 4) and launch campaigns to subvert congregations and denominations that historically embraced the apostolic Christian faith.

In America, wealth and business acumen have also been called upon to advance some of the most ancient and obvious falsehoods and errors. The Church of Latter Day Saints, better known as 'the Mormons', is a huge and highly profitable business enterprise devoted to promoting polytheism on a scale that rivals Hinduism, a 'gospel' of salvation by works righteousness, continuing revelation, 'baptism for the dead', 'eternal marriage', and a secret temple *cultus* modeled on Free Masonry.

Finally, we must reckon with the activity of Satan as 'the father of lies' (John 8:44). Wherever men call into question the truth and trustworthiness of God's Word, handle the Word of God deceitfully, and love and make a lie as a substitute for the truth of God's Word, we can see the hand of the enemy of souls at work.

DOWNES: How can a minister discern between those who are thinking their way through doctrines on the way to greater depth and clarity, and those who are questioning doctrines in a way that could lead to significant error?

BEEKE: First of all, we must follow the example of Christ and the apostles, who openly invited and urged their hearers to prove or test the truth and worth of what they proclaimed and taught. Reformed Christians have asserted and maintained the liberty of the Christian and the liberty of conscience. 'The requiring of an implicit faith, and an absolute and blind obedience, is to destroy liberty of conscience, and reason also' (Westminster Confession of Faith, 20.2).

Every minister must learn to defend the faith without being defensive or combative. 'The servant of the Lord must not strive; but be gentle unto all men, apt to teach, patient, in meekness instructing those that oppose themselves' (2 Tim. 2:24, 25a).

We should encourage our people to 'prove all things' (1 Thess. 5:21). Rather than rebuking someone for asking questions, we should devote our energy to finding answers to those questions from God's Word. The Ecumenical Creeds and Reformed Confessions, and the vast theological literature connected with them, are also great helps to a right under-standing of faith and practice.

On the other hand, as those who watch for the souls of God's people, we must be alert to any sign of straying from the truth. We must warn against embracing any notion or doctrine that requires one to set aside the clear testimony of Scripture. We must resist efforts to reinterpret Scripture in order to accommodate sinful practices or lifestyles. We must expose the sinful tendency of the fallen man to exalt himself and make himself a judge of God's Word, rather than submitting to its judgment.

We must use discernment. A true Christian will gladly receive faithful instruction from the Word of God. A man who is merely dabbling in theology or looking for an intel-lectual sparring partner deserves to be rebuked. And 'a man that is an heretic after the first and second admonition reject; knowing that he that is such is subverted, and sinneth, being condemned of himself' (Titus 3:10–11).

Downes: How do you cope with men who are sound in many ways, and whose ministries have been beneficial, but who, nonetheless, have held harmful views?

Beeke: One of the consequences, or benefits, of being known as a Reformed Christian who adheres consistently to the teaching of Scripture as summarized in the Reformed Confessions is that one is seldom put in such a position. Such men as you describe in your question seem to find the Reformed faith to be a pill they can't or won't swallow – perhaps because for all their strengths, these men are generally pragmatists and averse to consistency.

Even so, our people often find something attractive in the ministries of such men, and we need to take time to know their positions – both strengths and weaknesses – so that we can speak intelligently and helpfully about them. The diffi-culty is that these men and their ministries, broadcasts, and books are many and various. There is almost always one big name at a given moment, the man whose sayings and doings and nostrums are being widely discussed and hotly debated. We should beware of being drawn into endless and useless debates. These men come and go and have surprisingly little impact over the long term.

It should be a rule with us to have nothing to do with any man or ministry that errs in regard to the way of salvation in Jesus Christ. Whatever good a man may do along other lines, he has done the greatest conceivable harm if he errs at this point. 'It were better for him that a millstone were hanged about his neck, and that he were drowned in the depth of the sea' (Matt. 18:6).

DOWNES: Many Christians would be surprised to learn that major heretics like Pelagius and Faustus Socinus were known for scrupulously moral living, when perhaps they would have expected them to be openly immoral. How did Paul's assertion that false teaching leads to ungodliness manifest itself in the lives of these false teachers?

BEEKE: It is a misreading of Paul to suggest that false teaching must always lead to ungodliness or immorality, although it often does. Paul was keenly aware of the life he had lived as a Pharisee, so zealous to observe the traditions of the elders that he claimed to be 'touching the righteousness of the law, blameless' (Phil. 3:6). He likewise bears record of his fellow Jews that 'they have zeal of God, but not according to knowledge. For they being ignorant of God's righteousness, and going about to establish their own righteousness, have not submitted themselves unto the righteousness of God' (Rom. 10:2–3). It is simply a fact of human experience that men often do the right things for the wrong reasons.

It is therefore essential to the Christian notion of ethics to consider motive or 'the thoughts and intents of the heart' (Heb. 4:12), as well as outward appearance or conduct, when determining whether one's works are good or not. That which is not done out of true faith, in obedience to God's Word, and for the glory of God, is not, in the most important sense, a good work (Heidelberg Catechism, Q. 91). According to the Word of God, Pelagius and Faustus Socinus were both 'as an unclean thing', and all their good works were 'as filthy rags' (Isa. 64:6).

However much these men may have lived an outwardly moral life, Scripture describes them in very different terms: as 'grievous wolves ... speaking perverse things, to draw away disciples after them' (Acts 20:29–30). In the balance of Scripture, the sins of the mind and heart are more heinous than the sins of the flesh. It is gross wickedness to mislead others concerning the way of salvation, to destroy faith in the truth of God's Word, and to corrupt the worship of God.

At the same time, many Christians are guilty of failing to 'adorn the doctrine of God our Savior in all things' (Titus 2:9) – that is, by a consistent Christian manner of life and conduct. Because of the depravity that still cleaves to us, there must always be a gap between our profession and our conduct. We are called upon nonetheless to crucify the old nature, to walk in newness of life, and, in dependency on the Holy Spirit, to make every effort to narrow the gap between profession and conduct, for the sake of Christ and the gospel (cf. Rom. 8).

DOWNES: What would you consider to be the main theological dangers confronting us today, and how can we deal with them?

BEEKE: Some dangers have been with us for a long time, and some are just beginning to loom on the horizon. 'The Battle for the Bible' has been with us for more than one hundred years, and it has proven to be a great setback for the cause of Christ in the world. The apostasy of the Protestant churches in Europe and Great Britain; the disorder and corruption of evangelical churches in North America; the extension of much of that disorder and corruption to newly planted churches in Latin America, Africa, and Asia; the resilience of corrupt bodies such as the Church of Rome, and the sway it holds over so many millions; the propagation of cults of many kinds – all this may be attributed in very large measure to ignorance, false views, and rank unbelief concerning the unique character, content, and authority of Holy Scripture as God's written Word.

In the community of Reformed churches, we must deplore the rise of what can be called 'boutique' versions of the Reformed faith: little groups centered around some novel idea or practice, such as paedocommunion, that sets them apart from other Reformed Christians. Equally distressing is the widespread defection from the faithful observance of the Second Commandment regarding the regulation of the content and manner of Christian worship; many Reformed Christians have forgotten that the Reformers were as much concerned to regulate Christian worship according to Scripture as they were determined to establish Christian doctrine from the Word of God. Rightly understood and practiced, Christian worship is profoundly theological, spiritual and practical.

Nothing, however, is more astonishing than contemporary denials or disclaimers concerning faith as the sole instrument of our justification before God. Nothing was more basic to the Reformation, and nothing is more essential to the gospel, than justification by faith alone. Scripture acknowledges only one way of salvation, and it has nothing to do with covenant status, church membership, sacramental administration, Christian education, or progressive sanctification to acquire salvation. 'Believe on the Lord Jesus Christ, and thou shalt be saved' (Acts 16:31).

Almost as disturbing is the rise of the 'postmodern' school of thought or mind-set, and the inroads it is making among Christians in North America. As the name implies, postmodernism is a reaction to the modernism so dominant in Europe and America in the last decades of the nineteenth century and the first decades of the twentieth. One would think this rejection of modernism would work in favor of the historic Christian faith, but that is not the direction postmodernism has taken. Fundamental to postmodernism is the rejection of rational systems of thought and any kind of meta-narrative. Reformed Christianity has a rational system of thought, summarized in its historic creeds and confessions; its meta-narrative is nothing less than the witness of Holy Scripture to the history of redemption in Christ, and its summary in the gospel.

It is open to question whether there is any such thing as postmodernism, at least anything that can be expressed in positive terms. Even so, there are many important self-identified postmodern thinkers, writers and shapers of popular culture. Their blend of radical skepticism, unbelief, eclecticism and nihilism is making its impact on our world and the people to whom we must preach the gospel. It must also be admitted that these trends in the culture around us often have a profound and often destructive impact on the Christian church. We ministers should be alert to the ways in which the young people in our own churches, much more attuned to and involved in popular culture than we may like to think, may be embracing the stances and ways of postmodernism.

Knowledge is power, and we need to know and understand the world we live in and the churches we serve. Even more important, we need to grow in our knowledge and practice of the things taught and commanded in Holy Scripture. The man who knows the Scriptures well is 'throughly furnished unto all good works' (2 Tim. 3:16), including in particular the good work of proclaiming the great truths of the Christian faith, wielding God's Word as a mighty spiritual weapon, 'casting down imagination, and every high thing that exalteth itself against the knowledge of God' (2 Cor. 10:5) – in order to save both himself and his hearers and to build up the church of Christ unto all generations.

DOWNES: It is natural that a younger generation can find it harder to navigate the theological currents in the church. With all your ministerial experience, what advice would you give to younger ministers as they assess and handle various movements today?

BEEKE: Younger ministers are sometimes the victim of the particular bent of their theological training. Since the rise of the so-called 'Church Growth' movement, there has been an increasing emphasis on technique and methodology at the expense of the disciplines that once were the 'meat and potatoes' of seminary education, namely, biblical languages, exegesis, systematics, apologetics, church history, and the history of Christian doctrine.

Where this shift in emphasis has taken place, the seminary graduate will not have the tools he needs to use Scripture effectively and to wield it with ever-increasing knowledge and skill as 'the sword of the Spirit.' He will not have sufficient access to the Scriptures themselves, nor the comprehensive and analytical grasp of Christian truth, to be a true minister of the Word in today's world. He will find himself captive to the winds of the moment. As a preacher, he will be reduced to repeating the ideas of other men, gleaned from commentaries and popular books.

The minister who finds himself in this unhappy position should take action to make up for this deficit of knowledge and skill. He can go back to seminary and make a better choice of a place to train. He can seek advice and direction from other ministers and enter on a course of self-study. The important thing is for him to realize what he doesn't know and needs to know, and for him to seek out the best kind of books and study helps. Conferences and seminars are also helpful, and the guidance and encouragement of older and better-equipped ministers of the Word will be invaluable.

In sum, here are three short guidelines:

1. Become and stay well versed in the Scriptures, in confessional Reformed theology, and in the great classics of Reformed, experiential theology.

2. Summarize the errors of various movements succinctly from the pulpit when the scriptural text you are expounding pertains to them. Enlarge upon your exposure of error, perhaps, in catechism classes (because young people are

the church's future) or weekday classes (because those who attend have, in general, greater appreciation for apologetics than does your average Sabbath attendee and because your teaching situation is less formal).

3. Remember that you cannot study every false movement in depth, nor should you. Study in depth for yourself those that directly affect your congregation. Otherwise, read the best book from an evangelical perspective that refutes a particular error. In some cases, reading one good article may suffice.

Younger ministers should beware of being so caught up with the trends, debates, and crises of the present that they neglect to reinforce their knowledge of Christian history and Christian doctrine. It is important that they know what they are up against in terms of the challenges of today, but it is even more important that they know precisely what the Christian faith is at its roots, what the authentic gospel of Jesus Christ is, and how it is to be proclaimed, according to its Author. God does not change, His Word cannot change, His mercy is from everlasting to everlasting, and His Son, our Savior Jesus Christ, is the same yesterday, today, and forever.

CHAPTER EIGHTEEN

ERROR AND THE CHURCH

*An Interview
with Mike Ovey*

Mike Ovey has been Professor in the Doctrine, Apologetics and Liturgy department at Oak Hill College in England since 1998, where he currently serves as Principal. Since then has finished a Ph. D in the field of Trinitarian Theology. His most recent writing includes co-authoring *Pierced for Our Transgressions* with Andrew Sach and Steve Jeffrey.

MARTIN DOWNES: As you reflect back to your days in theological college and early years in the ministry were there men who started out with evangelical convictions who later moved away from the gospel? How did you cope with that?

MIKE OVEY: I would draw a distinction between those who very clearly moved away from the gospel in some way and those whose hearts became cold towards it. In the first category a very prominent evangelical leader with whom I had worked closely in a writing group announced that he was leaving his ministry because of his homosexual orientation. I and others found that enormously painful because of his giftedness in so many ways. I do think it faced some of us with the question of how much our own commitment had been tied to his leadership and how much rested simply in faith in the Lord Jesus. I found the best way of coping with this disappointment was to pray for my friend and for his restoration. I think that was what the rest of the writing group found as well. The great thing about that was that it helped us to continue to love our friend and not demonize him. And demonizing is, I think, the temptation that the fall of friends presents us with.

As regards those whose hearts grow cold, I think in a way this is even harder, simply because it is so difficult to spot. You meet a long-standing friend and you become aware not that there is a growing distance but that there is an established gulf. I give God great thanks that my closest friends from theological college have not had their hearts grow cold in this way, although over the years I have seen others of whom this would be true. Relationally, this is really very hard to handle because one has a sense of an elephant in the room and I'm not sure if I've established satisfactory patterns of dealing with this. I suspect the thing is not only to pray but to ask permission to speak and to describe fears. I guess the key question in such a conversation is to ask why someone has either stopped being evangelical or has grown cold towards the doctrines of grace. It's often said that much of the time the problem here is not so much an intellectual argument as a spiritual or moral struggle.

DOWNES: Have you ever been drawn toward any views or movements that time has shown to have been unhelpful or even dangerous theologically?

OVEY: No doubt I have been and no doubt I have been in ways of which I am not entirely aware. I think the fatal thing is to assume that one will not be drawn towards error at any time in one's ministry. If one makes that assumption then one starts to lose the possibility of self-correction, or more accurately God correcting us through the Scriptures. I think I am aware that my own views go through constant refinement, and I pray in the direction of orthodoxy rather than away from it.

DOWNES: How should a minister keep his own heart, mind and will from theological error?

OVEY: I think a minister must remember first that his mind is not a neutral instrument, but one that not infrequently will be used to rationalize his heart's desire. From that point of view there is a real need for a minister to concentrate on the fruit of the Spirit and in particular the virtues of humility and gentleness. It does seem to me that a heart that is prone to pride and aggression is likely to be prone to theological error. So spending personal time with the Lord, submitted to His Word, and where possible having an accountability group – all these things to my mind help protect us from theological error as well as from unholiness of life. The two do, I think, go together.

DOWNES: Calvin said that ministers have two voices. One is for the sheep and the other for warding off the wolves. How have you struck the right balance in this regard in your ministry?

OVEY: I don't think I always have struck the right balance between Calvin's two voices. One has to remember that in Acts 20, Paul tells us that some of the wolves will emerge from amongst our own numbers. To that extent, it is simply enormously difficult at times to spot whether someone is a wolf or a sheep and behave appropriately. In some ways, I suppose I would want to short-circuit this question and ask firstly whether what someone is saying or doing is true and biblical and secondly to try to exercise charity, whether they are a wolf or a sheep. But as one of the Anglican homilies (On Charity) puts it, charity on occasion involves correction and, if necessary, firm correction. That is equally true for a sheep as for a wolf.

DOWNES: Why do men possessed of fine intellectual gifts end up embracing and believing significant theological errors?

OVEY: I think there are three things that spring to mind. First, pride: in particular perhaps a pride of intellect that insists God should have said this rather than that, and therefore squeezes the Scripture into one's own system. Secondly, boredom: I think there is a spiritual malaise that has a sense of *ennui* at the presentation of simple gospel truths (Christ died for my sin, Christ rose again, He is the ascended Lord) and wants, so to speak, to explore the periphery of Christian theology. I think there is a cultural spirit in our time that loves the new and loves the esoteric. Thirdly, we can embrace error because we want to justify what we are doing: simple immorality over the years has led many of us astray.

DOWNES: Hilary of Poitiers said that 'Heresy lies in the sense assigned, not in the word written. The guilt is that of the expositor, not of the text.' What are the danger signs of this very thing happening in a man's ministry?

OVEY: I think the Hilary quote is brilliant. He also makes the point that a heretic uses the texts of Scripture but connects them in a way that the Scripture does not. Heretics do have an order, says Hilary (in respect of the Arian heresy), but the order is one that is imposed and is the heretic's own. To that extent I think Hilary is asking us not just to see if someone has an 'orderly' or 'coherent' exposition of Scripture, but whether the order and coherence is really one that the Scriptures establish.

DOWNES: How can a minister discern the difference between those who are thinking their way through doctrines on the way to greater depth and clarity, and those who are questioning doctrines in a way that could lead to significant error?

OVEY: I think a key pointer between those who want clarity and those who are questioning in a more dangerous way is whether the person in question is prepared to be corrected, and whether the person in question is content to say: 'The Scriptures take us this far and no further, so here I must rest.'

DOWNES: What are some of the consequences of a church, seminary or denomination tolerating false teachers?

OVEY: This is a hard one to answer. Any church, seminary or denomination will have a range of views. Some of those views will be wrong. Nevertheless there are some views which are so wrong that tolerating them takes the church, seminary or denomination beyond a critical mass, so to speak. When that happens, I think it's clear that error multiplies and will not be confined simply to the original mistake, and at a more fundamental level the tendency is for the organization in question to stop seeking truth and answers but to rest content with the existence of conflicting opinions. In that way the search for truth is a casualty and I feel that that leads to an exponential growth in problems.

DOWNES: Knowing that institutions tend to produce their opposite, and surely Princeton Seminary at one time a bastion of orthodoxy is a prime example of this, how can you humanly speaking maintain and safeguard the future of a theological college?

OVEY: People have tried all kinds of ways to safeguard theological colleges: trust deeds, limited finances, strict confessional adherence on the part of the faculty and so on. All of these are prone to failure both because the human heart is deceitful above all things, and I am sure Satan, the father of lies, wages active war against orthodox theological colleges and sometimes successfully sows deception amongst us. But we also have to admit that the custodians of our institutions will not always spot the problem at the time that it is most easily dealt with. All this means that we must exercise a certain ruthlessness with theological colleges and recognize that a great past is no justification for a present failure.

DOWNES: What would you consider to be the main theological dangers confronting us today and how can we deal with them?

OVEY: The attack on justification by faith is certainly one such danger. I think also the battle for the Bible never goes away. Obviously, the doctrine of penal substitution has been fairly consistently opposed over the last thirty years. Finally, I would strongly suspect that the uniqueness of Christ's person and His work are both under attack. I think these things need constant re-stating rather than assuming that they are held. Naturally, such re-statements have to take into account, where they can, the latest sets of criticism.

CHAPTER NINETEEN

WILL THE CHURCH STAND OR FALL?

An Interview on Justification and the New Perspective with Ligon Duncan

Ligon Duncan is the Senior Minister of the historic First Presbyterian Church (1837), Jackson, Mississippi, and Adjunct Professor at Reformed Theological Seminary. He is the author of *Fear Not*, and has edited the three volume series *The Westminster Confession into the 21st Century*.

MARTIN DOWNES: In his classic work on justification, James Buchanan begins by asserting that justification by faith appears to be a doctrine so well formed and stated that the case is closed on it. No one at the turn of the twenty-first century, looking at the academy and now even the church, would be able to take that view. Why has justification by faith alone become a contested doctrine again?

LIGON DUNCAN: I think that there are two main reasons for our current unsettlement on justification in the evangelical-reformed world. First, evangelicalism has been sub-biblical and sub-confessional in its understanding and preaching of the doctrine of justification (as expounded by the Reformers), especially in the last forty years, during which there has been (1) a general a-theological tendency and (2) preaching has been theologically anemic. Second, in the world of mainline academic biblical studies, historical-grammatical exegesis has been trumped by a tendency to allow tentative understandings of contemporaneous extra-biblical contextual material to dominate in the exegesis of the biblical text.

On the first point, I remember Sinclair Ferguson saying in a lecture a few years ago that whenever he hears someone going on about the 'new perspective' a little bubble pops up above his head that says 'I just wish they understood the old perspective.' It is a point well made, I think. Even in the confessional reformed community today we don't have a thorough grasp of the historic Protestant doctrine of justification the way our forebears did.

On the second point, it is a particular interpretation of extra-biblical material (from Second Temple Judaism) that has been appealed to in order to 'prove' that Paul is not criticizing legalistic Jewish soteriology, and therefore set exegetes free to search for a new understanding of Paul's teaching on justification that is consonant with what has been 'discovered' in the extra-scriptural sources. In my judgment, with as much Pauline material as we already possess, this is a heavy-handed and unreliable way of going about understanding Paul. If we only had one Pauline letter and no other New Testament material, then some sort of appeal to these extra-biblical sources in order to help figure out what Paul means might be understandable. But with the amount of Pauline literature that we have, to allow our necessarily tentative deductions from our study of secondary material override our understanding of the ample Pauline texts we have before us, is a dubious way of doing exegesis.

Now, let me quickly say that advocates of 'new perspectives' or 'fresh perspectives' on justification would give a simpler explanation in answer to your question. They would say that the reason the justification by faith alone has become a contested doctrine again, is because there is now a scholarly consensus that the Reformers (and late Medieval Roman Catholics) misunderstood Paul's teaching on the subject, and that research in the last thirty or so years has so improved our understanding of Paul that we must now abandon the 'old perspective' in favor of superior exegesis of the text. I believe that proponents of the new perspectives are wrong in this opinion, but it is (in general) the way they think about this issue.

DOWNES: What is attractive and plausible about the new perspectives on Paul?

DUNCAN: There are many answers to this question. Here are a few of them.

First, the new perspective (NPP), especially as articulated by N.T. Wright, claims to be superior exegetically in its interpretation of Paul to the old perspective. This why Wright, for instance, will insist that he is more 'reformed' than the defenders of reformed views on justification. Because he is simply following the text, while they are protecting their traditions. Thus, he is the true heir to the mantle of 'Sola Scriptura' not the tired protectors of the traditional Protestant dogma. Wright makes his case so intelligently and persuasively that his version of the NPP is plausible, and thus attractive to many evangelical scholars.

Second, and following on this first point, the NPP claims to set Paul's teaching in its original context, better than the old perspective does. The NPP's claim to offer a more accurate understanding of Paul by reading him in the context of Second Temple Judaism (rather than importing anachronistically the categories of later Medieval and early Reformation thought into him) appears plausible, and thus attractive to many evangelical scholars.

Third, the NPP, especially as articulated by N.T. Wright, admirably emphasizes the role of covenant theology in understanding Paul's thought. This is a helpful and needed corrective to some of the trends in NT scholarship prior to Sanders. Consequently, many evangelical and reformed scholars have found other aspects of the NPP plausible and therefore attractive.

Fourth, the NPP, especially as articulated by N.T. Wright, provides a more churchly, less individualistic reading of Paul than is typical in some evangelical circles (evangelicalism in general has been notoriously deficient in its doctrine of the church and heavily influenced by the individualism of late modernity). Evangelical scholars conscious of these deficiencies have sometimes (wrongly) blamed them on the theological legacy of the Reformation and thus have found the NPP a preferable and thus more attractive alternative to that tradition of exegesis.

Fifth, N.T. Wright is himself attractive. He is a highly intelligent, incredibly articulate, astoundingly prolific scholar and churchman. He has taken on liberals in the scholarly guild (valiantly defending cardinal Christian doctrines like the resurrection of Christ). He has embarked upon an almost singular project in contemporary mainstream NT studies (after all, who in the academy actually believes that there is such a thing as 'a theology' of the NT anymore?). Furthermore, he seems genuinely interested in engaging with and influencing evangelicals (while his more liberal colleagues simply heap scorn). All of this has, understandably, been attractive to evangelicals, and thus has made the NPP more attractive to some evangelicals.

Sixth, those in sympathy with the project of recasting Christian theology in light of our 'postmodern' context are often attracted to Wright's NPP views of eschatology and ethics, with his focus on the 'here and now', rather than the 'then and there' and on the social and structural entailments of the kingdom of God for Christians who want to live out the Lordship of Christ as intended by Jesus and Paul (as Wright sees it). Those who are inclined to blame the old perspective view of justification for stunted Christian social concern are apt to find in Wright's (and Dunn's) NPP views of justification a plausible and attractive alternative.

Seventh, evangelicals smitten with a re-casting of Christian theology via a narrative approach are attracted to Wright's breathtaking focus on the grand sweep of the Bible's story. His retelling of the gospel focuses on the global and cosmic mission of God, and seems bigger, grander, nobler and more victorious when stacked up against some evangelical constructions of the good news: God is coming to put the world to rights, not to rescue a handful of souls out of this world. God is reclaiming, redeeming and transforming His creation, not rapturing out a few spiritual survivors and abandoning the earth for a platonic refuge in heaven. To the extent that evangelicals find this vision exhilarating, they often find the NPP more plausible and thus attractive than its competitors.

More could be said, but that gives you a taste.

DOWNES: The New Perspectives are claimed to be the result of better exegesis of Paul and better awareness of the background to the New Testament. Is this really the case? Are there other factors at work?

DUNCAN: Well, no, I don't think so. Let me offer two problem areas for NPP exegesis.

1. The NPP's historical-contextual basis is dubious. Proponents of the NPP have drawn a questionable conclusion from the materials of Second Temple Judaism (2TJ). Personally, I believe that you can grant Sanders his own conclusions about the soteriology of 2TJ and still demonstrate that he has not successfully vindicated 2TJ from the charge of soteric legalism. This changes everything, if Sanders is wrong here.

2. The NPP's exegesis, for example, fails to do justice to Paul's vocabulary of justification. For Wright and others in the NPP, justification is all about covenant membership in God's Israel. But here's a test: (1) Find a lexicon which defines the Greek word *dikaiosune* ('righteousness') as 'membership within a group' or *dikaioo* ('justify') as 'to make or declare the member of a group.' You won't. (2)

Ask yourself, does Wright demonstrate, or does he simply assume or assert, that the Judaism contemporary to Paul viewed justification as all about covenant membership (in other words, that justification is all about knowing that you are 'in', rather than about being 'in' because you are acquitted and forgiven because of God's grace and by the work of the Messiah). He doesn't. No, when you consider the context that Paul himself gives you for understanding his teaching on justification, his train of thought when he's talking about justification, the words, phrases and concepts he compares and contrasts with it, and the other words he uses when he speaks of justification, then the 'traditional' Protestant view turns out to be exegetically superior.

Are there other factors at work? Yes, I think the NPP puts Paul in the straightjacket of an alien framework and makes what he is saying fit into that framework, no matter what. Ironically, this is precisely what NPP proponents accuse the Reformers of doing (but then again, NPP proponents don't understand the Reformers either!).

DOWNES: In your estimation why are these views dangerous?

DUNCAN: Well, one big reason they are dangerous is that they confuse people. The NPP formulations compromise the clarity of our grasp of the gospel, the freeness of grace, justification based on the alien righteousness of Christ, and the final basis of the assurance of the believer. And no greater tragedy could befall the church today than to compromise the lucidity of her preaching of the glorious gospel of grace. Nothing could be more tragic for ministers of the word than to be unsettled and unclear on the meaning of the gospel. Sadly, I've known more than one student enamored of the NPP and thus befuddled about how to articulate the gospel.

Second, the NPP views of Paul cannot adequately protect and sustain numerous aspects of the theology of sovereign grace to which we are the blessed heirs. The imputation of

Christ's penal and preceptive righteousness, his active and passive obedience to the believer – these things and more not only cannot be preserved by but are considered fictitious according to the NPP.

DOWNES: Why do you think N. T. Wright has had a much warmer reception in Reformed circles in the US compared to the UK?

DUNCAN: Well, in part because 'reformed' is defined more broadly in the US than the UK. The reformed and confessional community in Britain is more narrowly defined and more aware and appreciative of its historical and doctrinal roots than its broader cousins in the States. That being said, almost every NAPARC (North American Presbyterian and Reformed Council) denomination has publically and officially condemned or rejected the NPP. So, at least denominationally, the NPP has not been welcomed with open arms. However, in academic circles that are more broadly reformed and evangelical, both undergraduate and graduate, there is something of a buzz over N.T. Wright and the NPP. That is where Wright's reception has been warmest. By and large the lay people of the reformed community in the US are blissfully ignorant of his views on anything beyond the resurrection.

DOWNES: What is the Federal Vision and why has it caused such concern among Reformed churches?

DUNCAN: Well, those friendly with or involved in the Federal Vision (FV) would say that it is a conversation not a movement. But it has enough identifiable characteristics to be able to describe it. For some years now there has been a handful of voices on the margins of the American reformed community advocating for theological revision. Concerned that the reformed churches have been too influenced by revivalism and rationalism, and believing the traditional reformed doctrine itself has not escaped the blind-spots of its contexts, these men have articulated a need for reformed pastors and churches to undertake some serious theological reassessment. These voices speak from the periphery, and have not by and large reflected the theological outlook of the recognized evangelical and reformed seminaries nor the conservative reformed and presbyterian denominations, but a small sub-culture has grown up around these voices, and their message has been spread via the internet, weblogs, newsletters, self-published books, conferences, tapes/CDs/MP3 downloads and various other media. This diverse group of conversation partners has more recently embraced the designation 'Federal Vision' as a description of its collective aspirations. Among other things, they believe that classical Covenant Theology is in need of a biblical makeover and a fresh deployment in the reformed churches and in the lives of reformed Christians. Their proposals have not been widely embraced, but they have sparked controversy in the American reformed community.

Douglas Wilson of Moscow, Idaho (perhaps the best-known advocate of the FV, highlights the following as concerns of the FV: (1) to articulate and practice a more consistent view of the place of children in the covenant community and in relation to the promises of God [this often translates into the practice of paedo-communion in FV circles]; (2) to use language more biblically than has been the case, in their opinion, in traditional reformed dogmatics, as well as its desire to subject traditional, confessional systematic theology to a rigorous scriptural re-think [this often translates into FV proponents' dissatisfaction with confessional categories, formulations and boundaries]; (3) to coordinate the doctrine of union with Christ, with the doctrine of the Church, so as to correct what it sees as an errant distinction between (or at least an unhelpful deployment of the idea of) the visible and invisible church in traditional reformed ecclesiology [this sometimes results in FV proponents wanting to say that all members of the visible church are elect]; (4) to recover truths that the original reformers had discovered but which have been lost due to the influence of the Puritans and the Great

Awakening, not to mention revivalism [FV proponents tend to view Puritanism and the evangelical Calvinism of Whitfield and the Great Awakening as roots of numerous problems in the modern church]; and (5) to recast the doctrine of faith and obedience in more scriptural language and categories [because the FV does not think that the New Testament entertains the kind of opposition between faith and obedience that is often articulated in evangelical explanations of the relation between law and gospel, between faith and works]. Thus, FV advocates often express an interest in and concern for (1) sacramental efficacy, (2) the centrality of the visible Church, (3) the importance of a living and active faith in Christ, and (4) something they call 'real covenantal union with Christ.'

Why has the FV caused a concern in the reformed church in the US? Well, in the PCA for example, (1) **Because the FV has been promotive of church splits, and other ecclesiastical disruptions.** PCA presbyteries have refused to transfer PCA ministers sympathetic to the FV into their presbyteries, because they have found their views to be out of accord with our Confession of Faith and outside the pale of acceptable doctrinal opinion. Other NAPARC denominations have determined the same. Hence, the FV has been productive of ecclesiastical trials and the subject of denominational pronouncements. (2) **Because proponents of the FV are zealous to spread their views.** Consequently, NAPARC churches have appointed Study Committees and adopted position papers in order to check the spread of the FV errors. (3) **Because leading pastor-theologians in the Reformed and evangelical world have raised concerns over the unbiblical and anti-confessional views of the FV theology.** Sinclair Ferguson, Al Mohler, Doug Kelly, Brian Chapell, Don Carson, Rick Phillips, R.C. Sproul, Sean Lucas, Cal Beisner, Frank Barker and more have publicly indicated their disapproval of the theological program of some or all of these various figures and groups. Yet, **a not insignificant number of PCA teaching elders shows significant sympathy with**

these theological tendencies about which our most trusted churchmen and scholars have expressed distress.

DOWNES: What would be the impact on the life of a church and the life of a believer if they embraced the views of the covenant associated with forms of the Federal Vision and New Perspectives?

DUNCAN: The embrace of either the NPP or the FV (1) would require significant modifications of our public doctrinal commitments in confession reformed protestant bodies; (2) would bring confusion about the gospel, justification, assurance and the sacraments; (3) would open the door to a more thorough-going theological revision via the underlying hermeneutical principles in play; (4) for example, an acceptance of the whole package of N.T. Wright's views would expose a Christian or congregation to (a) a rejection of inerrancy; (b) the dismissal (or radical redefinition) of the historic Reformational understanding of key doctrines like justification, the imputation of Christ's righteousness to the believer, and the central message and mission of the church; (c) the embrace of women's ordination and gender egalitarianism; and (d) a very different view of the basis of Christian unity; and (5) for example, the embrace of the FV, could be promotive of (a) an unhealthy and unbiblical sacramentalism; (b) a confusion over the nature of justification and of saving faith; (c) an externalism and formalism; (d) a loss of assurance; (e) an undermining of the doctrine of the new birth; (f) a reconstructionist approach to Christian cultural engagement and more.

The biggest problem is the way these two movements or tendencies can impair and undermine vital religion, by the positive doctrinal errors they promote and the doctrinal confusion that they engender. One does not have to assert that those who are sympathetic to the NPP or FV are heretics doomed to perdition in order to indicate the problematic consequences of these views. It is always a dangerous thing to be incorrect, unclear or confused and confusing on gospel matters. Jonathan Edwards once made a wise observation on this, at the end of his own great messages on justification:

> How far a wonderful and mysterious agency of God's Spirit may so influence some men's hearts, that their practice in this regard may be contrary to their own principles, so that they shall not trust in their own righteousness, though they profess that men are justified by their own righteousness – or how far they may believe the doctrine of justification by men's own righteousness in general, and yet not believe it in a particular application of it to themselves – or how far that error which they may have been led into by education, or cunning sophistry of others, may yet be indeed contrary to the prevailing disposition of their hearts, and contrary to their practice – or how far some may seem to maintain a doctrine contrary to this gospel-doctrine of justification, that really do not, but only express themselves differently from others; or seem to oppose it through their misunderstanding of our expressions, or we of theirs, when indeed our real sentiments are the same in the main – or may seem to differ more than they do, by using terms that are without a precisely fixed and determinate meaning – or to be wide in their sentiments from this doctrine, for want of a distinct understanding of it; whose hearts, at the same time, entirely agree with it, and if once it was clearly explained to their understandings, would immediately close with it, and embrace it: – how far these things may be, I will not determine; but am fully persuaded that great allowances are to be made on these and such like accounts, in innumerable instances; though it is manifest, from what has been said,

> that the teaching and propagating [of] contrary
> doctrines and schemes, is of a pernicious and
> fatal tendency.

Edwards' point is worth pondering. Yes, we need to be ready to make great allowances for men's errors and inconsistencies, and to exercise the judgment of charity in connection with the state of their hearts, but we must also always remember that the teaching and promoting of doctrines and approaches to justification that are contrary to God's word are 'of a pernicious and fatal tendency.' They may lead sheep over the cliff.

DOWNES: Whenever a doctrine is under scrutiny and debate it is possible for church members to see weighty scholars on both sides and conclude that perhaps the issues aren't so clear cut. What would be the consequence of this for the status of the Reformed doctrine of justification? How can this confusion be overcome?

DUNCAN: It has always been thus. The great debates of ages past which now seem to us so clear-cut, were not so when they were first being hammered out. Arius claimed to be more biblical than Athanasius and the orthodox party at Nicea. Remember that, as John Murray often said: 'The difference between truth and error is not a chasm but a razor's edge.'

Another thing we need to factor into sorting out disputes is, what is the opinion of the church on this matter? Not simply what does this theologian or that theologian think, but what has the church officially and publically stated that it believes on this matter? This means that we will give more weight to creeds, confessions, and church statements of belief than we will to the views of individual scholars, however eminent they may be. This does not mean that we will put the church's confession on par with the Bible, nor that the church's confession is infallible and unimprovable. But it does mean that what the church has publically and officially confessed that it believes the Bible teaches, ought to carry more weight than the views of individual theologians.

Third, remember the doctrine of providence. Is it conceivable that the church has fundamentally misunderstood a doctrine close to the heart of the gospel for 2000 years until one man came along (N.T. Wright) who finally understands it? Or that Wright understands Paul better on justification and 'works of the law' than the post-apostolic fathers of the church (like, say, the writer of the Epistle to Diognetus)? I don't think so. By the way, this is not what Luther, Calvin and the other magisterial reformers claimed about their views. They claimed that their views were both more biblical and more consonant with the teaching of the early church than the views of their opponents.

DOWNES: What are the essential books, old and new, for pastors to read that faithfully articulate the doctrine of justification by faith alone?

DUNCAN: James Buchanan, *The Doctrine of Justification* (Edinburgh: Banner of Truth, 1867). This is the classic. Though written in the nineteenth century, it is amazing how Buchanan's study anticipates currents of the contemporary debate. J.I. Packer says: 'This is still the best text book on the subject, from the standpoint of the classic covenant theology.' And Roger Nicole opines: 'At the present stage of the justification debate, Buchanan would be a very wholesome remedy against unfair representations. He is absolutely masterful on the subject.'

K. Scott Oliphint, ed. *Justified In Christ: God's plan for us in justification* (Scotland: Mentor, 2007). Members of the Westminster Seminary faculty weigh in on this important subject. Stafford Carson shows how diluting justification endangers the truth of the gospel. Dick Gaffin spells out the relationship between justification and eschatology. Jeff Jue parallels the NPP and seventeenth century Arminianism. Pete Lillback on justification in various Reformation figures. Scott Oliphint on what is faith and in what sense is it related to justification. Lane Tipton on the importance of union with Christ. Carl Trueman on Christ's active and passive obedience. A good bibliography for further reading by Sandy Finlayson and an extensive introduction by Sinclair Ferguson.

John Fesko, *Justification: Understanding the Classic Reformed Doctrine* (Phillipsburg: P&R, 2008).

John is a good friend, colleague and sometimes sparring partner! He has been a Professor at RTS-Atlanta and Pastor of the Geneva OPC Church there. He is the newly-appointed Academic Dean of Westminster Seminary, California. This book is a comprehensive defense of justification by faith alone that treats several theological traditions and current exegetical, theological and ecumenical debates. His work includes discussion of the covenant of works, union with Christ, the New Perspective on Paul, Eastern Orthodoxy, and Roman Catholicism, and reflects this pastor-scholar's sensitivity to the important issues.

For understanding the NPP and N.T. Wright, let me suggest:

D.A. Carson & Douglas J. Moo, *An Introduction to the New Testament*. (Grand Rapids: Zondervan, 2005). Pages 375-385. Carson and Moo give a helpful ten page summary of the NPP and rejoin it from a classical Reformed evangelical perspective. Consider this the 'Cliff Notes' version of a reformed response to the NPP.

Counted Righteous in Christ: Should We Abandon the Imputation of Christ's Righteousness? (Wheaton: Crossway, 2002).

Piper here is mainly contending with Robert Gundry's denial of the classic doctrine of the imputation of Christ's righteousness to the believer, but the book is a well-rounded defense of the Bible's teaching on this vital subject, which also comes to play in NPP discussions.

The Future of Justification: A Response to N. T. Wright (Wheaton: Crossway, 2007). Here John Piper directly, painstakingly, carefully and charitably contests Wright's views. This is no light read. But if you get lost in the heavy-sledding in the middle of the book, go ahead and read the first and last chapters. This book was good enough that Wright thought he needed to write a response to it.

Guy Prentiss Waters' *Justification and the New Perspectives on Paul* (Phillipsburg, NJ: P&R, 2004). This is, perhaps, the best single book-length introduction and critique of the NPP. Written by a PCA minister, professor and scholar. Here's what the highly regarded New Testament Scholar Don Carson has to say about this book: 'In the last few years there have been several careful evaluations and critiques of the new perspective. This one excels for its combination of simplicity, fair dealing, historical awareness, and penetration. For the pastor who is vaguely aware of the debates, but who has little mastery of the confusing details, this book's careful presentation of each scholar's position is a model of accuracy and clarity. Even those who have been pondering the issues for years will see some things in a fresh light. The ability of Waters to combine exegetical, historical, biblical-theological and systematic reflections, and all in relatively brief compass, enhances the credibility of the argument. Combine these virtues with pedagogically helpful chapter summaries and an annotated bibliography, and it is easy to see why this book deserves wide circulation. In a domain where the issues are too important to ignore and where polarization is dividing congregations and denominations, it is a relief as well as a pleasure to come across a book noted much more for its light than its heat.'

Stephen Westerholm's *Perspectives Old and New on Paul: The 'Lutheran' Paul and His Critics* (Grand Rapids: Eerdmans, 2004). Here's where you go after Waters. Westerholm's revision of his 1988 *Israel's Law and the Church's Faith* is one of the most comprehensive and penetrating volumes addressing the NPP. Part One helpfully offers the reader summaries of Paul as Augustine, Luther, Calvin and Wesley have read him. Part Two updates Westerholm's 1988 survey of recent scholarship on Paul. Part Three expands and revises Westerholm's 1988 exegetical discussion of Paul's understanding of 'righteousness', 'law', and 'justification by faith'. The introduction will leave you on the floor laughing.

D.A. Carson, Peter T. O'Brien, and Mark A. Seifrid, eds. *Justification and Variegated Nomism, Volume Two: The Paradoxes of Paul* (Grand Rapids: Baker, 2004). This book is for the intrepid (so go ahead, get volume one as well!). Following the 2001 companion volume that addressed Second Temple Judaism, this volume concentrates on the biblical and theological issues touching the issues that the NPP have raised concerning the interpretation of Paul. Among the many fine essays in this volume are thorough exegetical studies of Romans 1:18-3:20 (Seifrid), Romans 3:21–4:25 (Gathercole), Romans 5–11 (Moo), and a treatment of Paul's language of faith and works in Galatians (M. Silva). O'Brien argues in two separate essays that Paul was not a covenantal nomist, and that Paul was called *and* converted at the Damascus Road. Yarbrough and Carson attempt positively to define Paul's relationship to the Old Covenant. T. George offers a contemporary defense of the Reformation's (and particularly Luther's) reading of the apostle Paul. Each student of the NPP should prioritize a careful reading of this volume. See especially Stephen Westerholm's chapter 'The "New Perspective" at Twenty-Five' – this essay competently surveys recent Pauline scholarship in the wake of Sanders' scholarship on ancient Judaism and Paul. It both abbreviates and supplements his overview of scholarship in the 2004 *Perspectives Old and New on Paul.* Westerholm in this essay and in *Perspectives* is especially helpful in grouping the works of contemporary Pauline scholars into 'families' of shared sympathies or similar approaches.

DOWNES: When engaged in polemics it does not take too long before strong words can be spoken against your character. The great New Testament scholar Gresham Machen was often vilified and subject to personal attacks. Why does this happen and how should you handle it?

DUNCAN: Expect it. Those who teach aberrant doctrine successfully are always, always possessed of two qualities – pride and intelligence. Both of these will often feature in their defense against critiques of their work.

Be determined to know their view (and to be able to articulate it) better than they know it themselves. If you cannot state the position of your opponent, in your own words, in a way in which they can recognize themselves, then you do not yet understand your opponent's position and you are not yet ready to enter into polemics with it. Following this counsel would, by the way, cut out 99 per cent of theological discussion on the internet!

Refuse to take the insults thrown back at you personally. You are a servant of the word. And if a servant, you must be prepared to be treated like a servant. The only thing that matters is the glory of God, the vindication of the word, the upholding of the truth, the faithful proclamation of the gospel and the good of souls. Let them cast what aspersions they may. You only crave the affirmation of One.

Roger Nicole and John Frame both offer good advice on how to engage in polemics.

DOWNES: Heresy is rarely presented in its true colors. Advocates always stress that their view is both biblical and pastorally beneficial. What principles should we follow to avoid being taken in by these schemes?

DUNCAN: Ask yourself questions about their view of Scripture. Whether they claim to have a high view of Scripture or not, do their views tend to undermine the final authority of the Bible.

Ask yourself questions about their doctrine of God. Do their views tend to undermine some aspect of His sovereignty or trinity?

Ask yourself questions about their doctrine of Christ. Do their views tend to undermine His claims of full humanity and full deity, or compromise the sole sufficiency and absolute necessity of His saving work?

Ask yourself questions about their doctrine of sin. Do their views deny original sin, or tend to undermine or scale down the sinfulness of humanity?

Ask yourself questions about their view of the gospel. Do they teach or imply a universalism? Do they compromise the sovereign initiative of God's grace in salvation? Do they find ways to incorporate man's deeds in his acceptance with God?

Ask yourself questions about their view of the church. Do they view the church as over the Bible or equal to the Bible, or do they realize that God's word brought the church into being and thus rules over the church? Do they view the sacraments as justifying or sanctifying? Do they acknowledge that the church has both visible and invisible aspects (that is, that there is an external and internal aspect to the church, and that the church is both local and extended in space and time)?

Ask yourself questions about their view of the end? Do their views promote escapism and retreat, or triumphalism and worldliness? Do they believe in the literal return of Christ? Do they believe in heaven/the age to come? Do they believe in the bodily resurrection and final judgment?

Ask yourself questions about their life. Do they show signs of humility or of spiritual pride? Do they bear the marks of the fruit of the Spirit? Has their teaching made them more humble, Christ-exalting, Scripture-obeying, world-denying, gospel-loving, people-serving, truth-treasuring and evidently submissive to proper spiritual authority?

Finally, (1) know your Bible; (2) know your church's confession or statement of faith; (3) know about the heresies of the past (because Satan is unoriginal).

By the way, many years ago the great Thomas Brooks made these seven observations about false teachers:

1. False teachers are men-pleasers. Galatians 1:10, 1 Thessalonians 2:1-4. They preach more to please the ear than to profit the heart. Isaiah 30:10, Jeremiah 5:30-31, 23:16-17.

2. False teachers are notable in casting dirt, scorn and reproach upon the persons, names and credits of Christ's most faithful ambassadors. 1 Kings 22:10-26, 2 Corinthians 10:10.

3. False teachers are venders of the devices and visions of their own heads and hearts. Jeremiah 14:14, 23:16, Matthew 24:4-5, 11:14, Titus 1:10, Romans 16:18.

4. False teachers easily pass over the great and weighty things both of law and gospel, and stand most upon those things that are of the least importance and concern to the souls of men. 1 Timothy 1:5-7, Matthew 23:23, 1 Timothy 6:3-5, Romans 2:22.

5. False teachers cover and color their dangerous principles and soul-deceptions with very fair speeches and plausible pretenses, with high notions and golden expressions. Do not be 'bewitched and deceived by the magnificent words, lofty strains, and stately terms of deceivers.' Galatians 6:12, 2 Corinthians 11:13-15, Romans 16:17-18, Matthew 16:6, 11-12, 7:15.

6. False teachers strive more to win over men to their opinions, than to better them in their lives. Matthew 23:15.

7. False teachers make merchandise of their followers. 2 Peter 2:1-3, Revelation 18:11-13, Jeremiah 6:13.

DOWNES: If the doctrine of justification by faith alone is still the doctrine by which the church stands or falls what are your hopes and fears for evangelicalism and for confessionally Reformed churches on this very point?

DUNCAN: I do not fear and I am deeply concerned.

I do not fear. The Lord will build His church, and even the very gates of hell will not be able to resist the onslaught of the kingdom.

That being said, I am deeply concerned. The spirit of the age is compromise and defection. What is required of ministers in times of spiritual unfaithfulness and doctrinal downgrade and defection is steadfast, unyielding devotion to the truth.

We must stand fast. And we must out-live, out-rejoice, out-love, out-preach, out-serve and out-die the false teachers and errorists.

And I am cautiously optimistic. Even in the short run. The so-called 'young, restless and Reformed' crowd shows many evidences of resisting the 'justification downgrade'. Hang in there, brothers!

CHAPTER TWENTY

THE ANNIHILATION OF HELL

*An Interview
on Evangelicals and Eternal Punishment
with Robert Peterson*

Robert A. Peterson, Ph.D, Professor of Systematic Theology, Covenant Theological Seminary, St. Louis, Missouri. He is the author of *Hell on Trial: The Case for Eternal Punishment*, and has co-edited with Chris Morgan *Hell Under Fire* and *Faith Comes By Hearing*.

MARTIN DOWNES: How did you arrive at your convictions on the doctrine of hell and why has this become a doctrine that you have sought to defend and teach?

ROBERT PETERSON: In order to answer this question it is necessary first to define some key terms concerning the eternal destiny of human beings.

Universalism is the view that eventually everyone will be saved. For good biblical and theological reasons, this view has been held by few believers in the history of the church. Jesus' words in Matthew 18:6–9; 25:31–46; Mark 9:42–48; and His apostles' teaching in 2 Thessalonians 1:5–10; Jude 7, 13; and Revelation 14:9–11; 20:10, 14–15 have caused those with a high view of Scripture to reject universalism.

Postmortem evangelism, also called eschatological evangelism, is the view that at least some human beings will be given an opportunity after death to believe the gospel and be saved. Although a small number of evangelical scholars of various traditions espouse this view today, John 8:21, 24 and Hebrews 9:27 contradict it.

Annihilationism, as held by some evangelicals, is to be distinguished from mortalism, the view that at death the dead cease to exist. Mortalism is contradicted by Scripture's clear teaching in both testaments that the dead will be raised (Dan. 12:2; John 5:28–29; Acts 24:15; Rev. 20:11–15). Evangelical annihilationists agree with the historic view of the church up to a point: Christ will return, the dead will be raised, the Last Judgment will occur, and the unsaved will be cast into hell, where they will pay the penalty for their sins. Unlike orthodoxy, however, annihilationism maintains that the unsaved will pay that penalty over a shorter or longer time, and then they will suffer the last stroke – the extinction of their being, which is said to be the worst possible fate. The more popular term for this view today is conditional immortality, or **conditionalism** for short, which holds that God, who alone possesses immortality inherently (which is correct; 1 Tim. 6:16), does not give immortality to all human beings (which is incorrect in light of Matt. 25:34, 41, 46, to cite one passage), but only to those whom He regenerates. Those who die unsaved, and therefore lack immortality, will eventually cease to exist.

Traditionalism is the historic view of the Christian church, having been held by Tertullian, Augustine, Aquinas, Luther, Calvin and Edwards, as well as twentieth-century evangelicals who wrote standard systematic theologies for various traditions: Francis Pieper (Lutheran), Louis Berkhof (Reformed), Lewis Sperry Chafer (dispensationalist), and Millard Erickson (Baptist). The historic view holds that the wicked will suffer eternal conscious punishment at the hands of the living God.

Although I received the doctrine of hell as a part of my seminary education, I did not begin to examine it critically until I came into contact with writers espousing the aberrant views expressed above. I took those views very seriously and found them lacking as I taught on the topic of eternal destinies and wrote *Hell on Trial: The Case for Eternal Punishment* in 1995. I became increasingly aware that whereas in the history of the church attacks on the doctrine of hell largely came from outside the church, in recent times that situation has been changing. From within the church, Christians, including numbers of evangelicals, have been rejecting traditionalism for conditionalism, with a few inclined toward postmortem evangelism, and a very few even teaching universalism.

Out of a concern for the truth, I wrote rejecting these views and in defense of the orthodox historic position. I debated conditionalist (annihilationist) Edward Fudge in *Two Views of Hell: A Biblical and Theological Dialogue* (InterVarsity, 2000). In 2004 I co-edited with Christopher Morgan *Hell under Fire: Modern Scholarship Reinvents Eternal Punishment* (Zondervan, 2004). Here Albert Mohler sounds the alarm concerning false views of hell today, J. I. Packer opposes universalism and Chris Morgan refutes annihilationism.

DOWNES: Could you state briefly the essential outlines of the doctrine of hell and some of the key texts where it is taught?

PETERSON: The main outlines of the Bible's teaching on the Last Judgment, which issues in the eternal destinies of heaven (more precisely eternal life with God and all of the resurrected saints on the new earth) and hell include its timing, purposes, and circumstances.

The *timing* of the Last Judgment. It will occur at the end of the age (Matt. 13:40–43), after Christ's second coming (Matt. 25:31–32, 34, 41, 46), after the resurrection of the dead (Rev. 20:12–13), and before the new heavens and the new earth (2 Pet. 3:7–13).

The *purposes* of the Last Judgment are three. These are, first and foremost, to display the glory of God in the salvation of His people and damnation of the wicked. That day will reveal His sovereignty, righteousness, power, truth and holiness (Rom. 2:5; Rev. 11:17–18; 15:3–4; 16:5–6). Second, the Judgment will not *determine* eternal destinies; they are determined before death by people's relation to Christ (John 3:16–18). Rather, the Judgment will *assign* those destinies (John 5:27–29). Third, the Judgment will reveal degrees of reward and punishment (Matt. 11:22–24; Luke 12:47–48; 19:16–19; Rom. 2:5; 1 Cor. 3:12–15).

The *circumstances* of the Last Judgment are three. First, God will be the Judge. Sometimes, Scripture attributes the work of the final judgment to the Father (e.g., Rom. 14:10; 1 Pet. 1:17), sometimes to the Son (e.g., Matt. 16:27; John 5:22), and never to the Holy Spirit. But because God is the holy Trinity and the three persons are inseparable, it is best to say that the final Judgment will be performed by the Trinity, especially the Father and Son.

Second, angels and all human beings will be judged. Scripture teaches the judgment of angels (1 Cor. 6:2–3; 2 Pet. 2:4; Jude 6). It also teaches the judgment of all human beings (Rom. 2:5–6; 3:6; Rev. 20:12–13).

Third, contrary to what many assume, the Last Judgment will not be based on faith or lack of faith, but on what people have done, which reveals their faith or lack of faith. Judgment is based on thoughts (1 Cor. 4:5), words (Matt. 12:36) and deeds (2 Cor. 5:10; Rev. 20:12–13). It is not difficult to understand that it is just for God to deal with the lost in this way. He does not condemn them because they have not heard of Jesus (although Jesus is the only way to salvation: John 14:6; Acts 4:31). Instead, they are condemned for their sins and have no protest as to the justice of their condemnation.

The problem, of course, is the judgment of the righteous based on deeds. It is important to see how clear this is in Scripture – Psalm 62:12; Matthew 16:27; John 5:28–29; Romans 2:6–11

– and to see that even these deeds are a part of the salvation by grace given to God's people. These deeds are the work of the Father (Phil. 2:12–13), done by abiding in the Son, apart from whom we can do nothing pleasing to God (John 15:5), and they are the fruit of the Holy Spirit (Gal. 5:22–23).

DOWNES: Will you demonstrate from Scripture why the church through the ages has held that hell involves never-ending punishment for unsaved human beings?

PETERSON: Jesus condemns people who do not take precautions to avoid being 'thrown into the eternal fire ... the hell of fire' (Matt. 18:8, 9 ESV). Though the word rendered 'eternal' (*aionios*) can mean 'age-long', it should be translated 'eternal' when speaking of final destinies, because these destinies pertain to the age to come, an age that is qualified by the very life of God Himself. The age to come lasts as long as God does – forever.

In Mark 9 Jesus again teaches that hell is without end. Unsaved persons are in danger of going 'to hell to the unquenchable fire ... where their worm does not die, and the fire is not quenched' (vv. 43, 48 ESV). In our experience, every fire goes out when its fuel is exhausted, and every worm dies when it has no more food. It will not be so in the life to come; there fire and worm never cease. This is metaphorical language for the everlastingness of hell.

In the most famous passage dealing with hell (Matt. 25:31–46), Jesus twice teaches hell's eternal duration. First, He consigns the wicked to 'the eternal fire prepared for the devil and his angels' (Matt. 25:41 ESV). What Jesus here labels 'eternal', His apostle John says means being 'tormented day and night forever and ever' (Rev. 20:10 ESV). Plainly, hell is endless.

Second, Jesus places the fates of the wicked and the righteous alongside each other. 'Then these will go away into eternal punishment, but the righteous into eternal life' (Matt. 25:46 ESV). The parallelism shows that the pain of the lost and the joy of the saved both last forever.

Paul teaches the same thing when he says that the lost will experience 'eternal destruction' which involves being 'away from the presence of the Lord' (2 Thess 1:9 ESV). 'Eternal destruction' is not annihilation, for the lost must continue to exist to be shut out from the Lord's presence. Rather, 'eternal destruction' means total ruin.

Jude teaches that hell is endless when he paints images of fire and darkness to describe the destiny of the godless. The wicked will undergo 'a punishment of eternal fire' and are 'wandering stars for whom the gloom of utter darkness has been reserved forever' (vv. 7, 13 ESV).

The Book of Revelation teaches that the unsaved will suffer eternal torment. 'And the smoke of their torment goes up forever and ever. They have no rest day or night' (Rev. 14:11 ESV). The fact that the smoke rises forever indicates that the fire still has fuel. It is not a picture, then, of extinction, but of endless punishment.

When John says that the damned have 'no rest day or night' (Rev. 14:11 ESV), he implies their ongoing existence. If annihilation were true, it would provide rest for the wicked; they would cease to exist and experience no more pain. But since they have no relief from the unrelenting wrath of God their punishment is everlasting.

John's employment of the images of 'the lake of fire' and 'the second death' say the same thing. Twice John equates 'the second death' with 'the lake of fire' (Rev. 20:14; 21:8 ESV). He uses the symbol of 'the lake of fire' five times. The first time, he says that the beast and the false prophet are thrown alive into the lake of fire (Rev. 19:20 ESV). Later the devil is thrown in, joining the other two for eternal torment (Rev. 20:10). Still later, lost human beings are thrown into the lake of fire (Rev. 20:14-15). John discloses the finality and universality of the Final Judgment when he says that the sea and death and Hades yielded up the dead that were in them (v. 13). In fact, death and Hades themselves 'were thrown into the lake of fire' (v. 14 ESV). Death and the grave (the intermediate state) thus give way to the lake of fire, the second death (the final state).

Annihilationists err, therefore, when they claim that the second death and the lake of fire signify the extinction of the wicked. On the contrary, John specifically says that the punishment of the lake of fire lasts 'day and night forever and ever' (Rev. 20:10 ESV).

Scriptural evidence for eternal conscious torment is not lacking. Some, however, are unwilling to accept it.

DOWNES: Why has there been a willingness by some evangelicals in the last one hundred years or so to accept and embrace annihilationalism?

PETERSON: Though some annihilationists insist that the Bible alone has motivated their rejection of the historic doctrine, others admit that emotional considerations have played a part. Without judging the motives of individuals, my opinion is that the intellectual and emotional climate of our times has more to do with the move away from some historic doctrines, including that of hell, than many realize. In an increasingly pluralistic culture, it is politically incorrect to hold that people who do not trust Christ as Lord and Savior, will suffer everlasting torment in body and soul. But that is exactly what the Bible teaches. (For a recent defense of exclusivism, the view that one must hear and believe the gospel of Christ in this life to be saved, see, C. W. Morgan and R. A. Peterson, *Faith Comes by Hearing: A Response to Inclusivism* (InterVarsity, 2008).

Perhaps the candid response of one employee of an Evangelical publisher, when asked what she thought of a book featuring a debate between traditionalism and annihilationism, reflects the default mode of many: 'I certainly hope that annihilationism is true!' It is not our place to hope that certain things are true with reference to the things of God. It is our place to humbly receive the Word that God has given. That means restraining our curiosity where the Word is silent. And that means believing and obeying God's truth even if we don't like it. Two orthodox doctrines that became immediate targets for 'liberated' human reason in the Enlightenment – original sin and eternal conscious punishment for the lost – are not my favorites. But the Word of God teaches them and so I am obligated to receive them as true and to live accordingly.

I am afraid that too many people today reach conclusions as to what they believe concerning the Christian faith on the basis of their feelings and desires rather than the teaching of Scripture. As J. I. Packer remarked some years ago: 'If you want to see folk damned something is wrong with you!' Of course this is true, but Packer went on to say that some of God's truth is hard and one such truth is the Bible's teaching concerning eternal hell.

It seems to me that the hard words of D. A. Carson are correct: 'Despite the sincerity of their motives, one wonders more than a little to what extent the growing popularity of various forms of annihilationism and conditional immortality are a reflection of this age of pluralism. It is getting harder and harder to be faithful to the "hard lines" of Scripture' (*The Gagging of God: Christianity Confronts Pluralism* [Zondervan, 1996], 536). But the Lord requires nothing less of us than, by His grace, to be faithful.

DOWNES: Those who deny eternal punishment appeal to an inappropriate use of metaphorical language by advocates of the more traditional view of the doctrine. What is the relationship between Scripture's use of metaphors for hell and literal descriptions?

PETERSON: The Bible uses metaphorical language to talk about both heaven and hell. Jesus' words to Nicodemus hint as to why: 'If I have told you earthly things and you do not believe, how can you believe if I tell you heavenly things?' (John 3:12 ESV). The 'earthly things' that Jesus told Nicodemus are the new birth! It is earthly, not in its origin, but because of where it takes place. Jesus means that Nicodemus, and we, would have no ability to understand if He spoke directly of what was going on in His Father's presence in heaven.

Matters of heaven and hell are far beyond us, so God graciously speaks to us of them in terms we can understand. That is why He describes heaven as a garden, a city, a family, a banquet, a river, and so on. He cannot speak to us literally of unseen things because we would not comprehend. So He stoops to our weakness and ignorance, and uses metaphors to communicate to us the reality of everlasting bliss with Him and all of God's people on the new earth.

So it is with hell. God communicates to us the reality of unending suffering of the lost by using metaphors – of fire, darkness, being cut in pieces, destruction, loss, and separation. At times He uses plain words – 'weeping and gnashing of teeth' – so that we do not miss the meaning of the metaphors; they speak of horrible pain.

Jesus, the only Savior of humankind, spoke the most about hell in Scripture and rightly so. Only He is qualified to speak the most about the unspeakable. Seven times Jesus speaks of 'weeping and gnashing of teeth' (in Matt. 8:12; 13:42, 50; 22:13; 24:51; 25:30; Luke 13:28 ESV). Make no mistake, the words speak of 'extreme suffering and remorse' (*The New International Dictionary of Theology*, ed. Colin Brown, 3 vols., [Zondervan, 1976], 2:421). Jesus uses this phrase twice to help explain the meaning of being thrown 'into the fiery furnace' (Matt. 13:42, 50 ESV). Four times He uses the expression to explain the ideas of darkness and separation (Matt. 8:12; 22:13; 25:30; Luke 13:28).

This image, therefore, ties together many others. If anyone is still unconvinced that Scripture uses metaphorical language to speak of hell, they should hear Jesus' words: to the unprepared servant, the Master says, he 'will cut him in pieces and put him with the hypocrites. In that place there will be weeping and gnashing of teeth' (Matt. 24:51 ESV). I know of no one who holds that the unsaved will literally be cut to pieces in hell. Rather, both testaments speak figuratively of severe punishment as being cut in pieces (Deut. 32:41; Heb. 11:37). Jesus does not leave us guessing about the nature of hell. He uses metaphors with which we are familiar to describe that with which we are unfamiliar – a place of unimaginable suffering.

DOWNES: Can one accept wholeheartedly annihilationist views of hell and remain consistently evangelical?

PETERSON: After thinking about these kinds of questions for some years, here are my views. I have been asked more than once if, in my opinion, someone holding to annihilationism can become a member of a church in the Presbyterian Church in America (in which I am an ordained minister). My answer is that such a person may be a member in good standing of a PCA church but not hold church office. This is because Scripture requires that a person believe in Christ as Lord and Savior to be a church member, but has higher qualifications for church office. Deacons, in addition to faith in Christ, 'must hold the mystery of the faith with a clear conscience,' (1 Tim. 3:9 ESV) and elders, in addition to faith in Christ, 'must hold firm to the trustworthy word as taught' (Titus 1:9 ESV).

Can one accept wholeheartedly annihilationist views of hell and remain consistently evangelical? One can hold such views and remain evangelical, but I question the consistency of such a view with evangelicalism, so my answer is no.

DOWNES: If one embraces a belief in annihilationist views of hell what effects does this have on other key doctrines? What practical effects does this carry?

PETERSON: The answer is that annihilationist views sometimes affect other key doctrines and sometimes do not. To the best of my knowledge, John Stott, who tentatively defended annihilationism in 1988, admitting that he had privately held it for years, commits an isolated error. That is, his annihilationism does not affect other doctrines in his system of theology.

But, Edward Fudge, whom I debated in the 2000 IVP book *Two Views on Hell*, commits a systemic error. That is, his annihilationist views affect other matters in his doctrinal system. He correctly argues that Christ suffered the pains of hell on the cross. But then he assumes those pains are annihilation and teaches that 'Jesus' death involved total destruction' (*The Fire That Consumes: A Biblical and Historical Study of Final Punishment*, 228–34). This is an error that causes confusion with his view of Christ's person. When I asked Fudge to define the annihilationism that Christ's death entailed, he refused. But it seems that either the whole person of Christ would have had to have been destroyed or at least His humanity (See *Two Views of Hell: A Biblical and Theological Dialogue*, 174–79). These repercussions are serious and should cause Fudge to rethink his view that Christ suffered annihilation on the cross, and furthermore, that annihilation is the fate of the lost.

It seems to me that to be annihilated and thus 'put out of one's misery' is not that bad a fate, especially compared to everlasting suffering. I hope that Christians and churches that forsake the historic view of hell for annihilationist views will not experience a lessening of urgency to preach the gospel and support missions. I question whether unsaved persons who hear the gospel combined with annihilationism will fear that fate as sinners historically have feared going to hell. I am not saying that the fear of hell is the only motivation for believing the gospel. But I know that it has been one powerful motivation for many.

DOWNES: In your experience what has been the status of the doctrine of hell among church members and in the thinking of those training to be pastors?

PETERSON: I have been active in local evangelical churches for forty years and in the training of pastors for thirty.

Unfortunately, in my experience, the doctrine of hell has been neglected among church members and even in the thinking of those training to be pastors. The words of Lesslie Newbigin are truer today than when he penned them in 1994: 'It is one of the weaknesses of a great deal of contemporary Christianity that we do not speak of the last judgment and of the possibility of being finally lost' ('Confessing Christ in a Multi-Religion Society,' *Scottish Bulletin of Evangelical Theology* 12 [1994]: 130–31, quoted in Carson, *The Gagging of God*, 536). Part of the blame should be placed at the feet of evangelical pastors, who surveys show have been slow to teach and preach what the Bible says about hell. My study of hell in the mid-1990s brought me to repentance because I was personally guilty of such neglect. My experience has been that if we can bring hell to evangelicals' minds and hearts, if we can move it from being a passive to an active doctrine, then they will begin to pray about their lost friends and loved ones as never before. That in turn motivates them to share the gospel as the Holy Spirit leads. And that produces fruit in terms of spiritual growth in the lives of the evangelists and salvation for some of those evangelized.

DOWNES: How should the doctrine of hell be preached

PETERSON: It should be preached by pastors who have a deep sense of Christ's redeeming them from hell (see Sinclair B. Ferguson, 'Pastoral Theology: The Preacher and Hell' in *Hell under Fire*, 219–37). Such pastors must prayerfully, lovingly and faithfully share the message of Jesus, the Redeemer of the world, and His apostles that those who die in their sins will suffer 'eternal punishment' (Matt. 25:46 ESV), even 'the punishment of eternal destruction away from the presence of the Lord and from the glory of His might' (2 Thess. 1:9 ESV). At times I have found it impossible not to weep as I speak of Christ suffering the pains of hell, of drinking the cup of God's wrath for us, so that we do not have to do so. The Bible's message of hell is a topic worthy of study, but in addition, it has to be something that moves us to action – to repentance, when we consider what our sins deserve; to prayer, out of compassion for the lost; to worship, when we consider what Christ endured to redeem us; and certainly, to witness, when we desire for others to know our great God and Savior.

DOWNES: What are some of the most significant books on the doctrine of hell that every church leader or concerned Christian should know about?

PETERSON: The doctrine of hell belongs to the area of theology known as eschatology, or the study of last things. Two books giving a solid overview of last things are Anthony A. Hoekema's *The Bible and the Future* (Eerdmans, 1979) and Cornelis Venema's *The Promise of the Future* (Banner of Truth Trust, 2000).

Worthwhile books treating both destinies include Bruce Milne's *The Message of Heaven and Hell: Grace and Destiny* (The Bible Speaks Today; InterVarsity, 2002) and Peter Toon's *Heaven and Hell: A Biblical and Theological Overview* (Nelson, 1986).

An important book that sounds the alarm concerning a weakening of evangelical theology, including the move away from eternal punishment, is D. A. Carson's *The Gagging of God: Christianity Confronts Pluralism* (Zondervan, 1996).

On the debate between annihilationism (conditionalism) and the traditional view of hell, see the volume by the Evangelical Alliance Commission on Unity and Truth Among Evangelicals (ACUTE): *The Nature of Hell* (ACUTE/Paternoster, 2000). The standard conditionalist text today is Edward William Fudge's *The Fire That Consumes: A Biblical and Historical Study of Final Punishment* (Providential Press, 1982). I debate Fudge in *Two Views of Hell: A Biblical and Theological Dialogue* (InterVarsity, 2000).

A classic defense of eternal punishment is William G. T. Shedd's *The Doctrine of Endless Punishment* (Charles Scribner's Sons, 1886; reprint, Klock & Klock, 1980). A good popular book presenting the traditional view is Larry Dixon's *The Other Side of the Good News: Confronting the Contemporary Challenges to Jesus' Teaching on Hell* (Christian Focus, 2003). My *Hell on Trial* (mentioned above) is used as an introductory textbook by some Bible colleges and seminaries. A useful work on a key historical figure is Christopher W. Morgan's *Jonathan Edwards and Hell* (Christian Focus, 2004).

The best academic book on hell today is one that I co-edited with Christopher Morgan, titled, *Hell under Fire: Modern Scholarship Reinvents Eternal Punishment* (Zondervan, 2004). It contains essays by notable evangelical scholars, including Gregory Beale, Daniel Block, Sinclair Ferguson, Albert Mohler, Douglas Moo, J. I. Packer, and Robert Yarbrough.

I thank Chris Morgan, my writing partner, for offering comments and Rick Matt, my staff colleague at Covenant Seminary for helpful editing.

CHAPTER TWENTY-ONE

THE WORD OF TRUTH

*An Interview on Inerrancy
with Greg Beale*

Unlike the other interviews in this volume, which were all entirely conducted in a written format, this interview was carried out by telephone. What follows is an edited transcription.

Greg Beale is Professor of New Testament and Chair of Biblical Studies at Wheaton College, Illinois. He is the author of several books including *The Erosion of Inerrancy in Evangelicalism*, *We Become What We Worship*, and *The Book of Revelation: A Commentary on the Greek Text*. Professor Beale has also edited, along with D.A. Carson, *Commentary on the New Testament use of the Old Testament*.

MARTIN DOWNES: Why do you believe that the Bible, as originally given, is not only inspired but also inerrant?

GREG BEALE: It is intriguing that some people don't like the term 'inerrancy' because it sounds too negative. They also say the word cannot be found in Scripture. But you do find the concept. For example in John 10:35 Christ says that Scripture cannot be broken. And of course there are the well-known texts like 2 Timothy 3:16, 'All Scripture is God-breathed' and 2 Peter 1:21 'prophecy never had its origin in the will of man, but men spoke from God as they were carried along by the Holy Spirit.'

The traditional syllogism of classic orthodox evangelicalism is that since God is true and without error, His oral Word is true and without error, and when His oral Word becomes inscripturated it is therefore true and without error. This syllogism has been challenged most recently by Andrew McGowan in his book *The Divine Spiration of Scripture*. McGowan argues that this syllogism is not biblical. I'm prepared to argue that it is not only biblical but that it is also exegetical (on which see further below).

Downes: What are some of the principle exegetical foundations of inerrancy?

Beale: As I mentioned, I believe that the concept of inerrancy is in Scripture. The syllogism that I referred to is found in some parts of the Bible, even though McGowan says that there is no evidence of such an exegetical syllogism but that it is an assumption imposed on the Scriptures.

You can, however, see this syllogism in the book of Revelation. I began to reflect on this when McGowan issued this challenge. Part of what I am now going to summarize can also be found partly in my commentary on Revelation. The key texts are Revelation 3:14 , 21:5, and 22:6.

In Revelation 3:14 Christ introduces Himself and says He is 'the Amen, the faithful and true witness'. Now, it is acknowledged by most commentators that the Amen comes from Isaiah 65:16. This is the only place in Scripture where 'Amen' is a name. And it is a name for God. He is the 'Amen', and He is called the 'Amen' twice there in Isaiah 65:16. Christ expands that into 'the Amen, the faithful and true witness'. That extension by the way is found in different LXX versions of Isaiah 65:16 and so there is already a precedent for expanding 'Amen' in the way Jesus Himself does in Revelation 3:14.

We have here an identification Christology. Christ is Yahweh. It is a wonderful Christological text. He says 'the Amen, the faithful and true witness, the beginning of the creation of God' (the latter phrase probably coming out of Isaiah 65:17 which says, 'Behold, I create new heavens and a new earth.' Jesus' resurrection is the beginning of that new creation).

So now Christ is speaking, and He is 'faithful and true'. Therefore He can be depended upon in His oral Word. But this oral Word is inscripturated here, and so it too can be depended upon. Especially since it ends with, 'He who has an ear, let him hear what the Spirit says to the churches' in 3:22. These are the words of Christ and they are the words of the Spirit, which John has been commanded to 'write'. But at this point let us be satisfied merely to say that Christ's oral Word here is faithful because He is seen as a faithful witness.

His character is faithful and true, therefore as God was called the 'Amen, the faithful and true' (putting the different Septuagintal traditions of Isaiah 65:16 together), Christ identifies Himself as 'the Amen, the faithful and true witness'. His witness is faithful and true, and what He says is faithful and true. Very intriguingly, in Revelation 21:5 we have this statement: 'He who sits on the throne says, "Behold, I'm making all things new."' Here we have the new creation again, and He says, 'Write, for these words are faithful and true.'

Here we have a development from 3:14, but it still has in mind Isaiah 65:16. But now, notice, this is not Christ who is faithful and true. What is happening here is that, what was true of Yahweh and Jesus – that their character is faithful and true – is now being taken and applied to written scriptural form in the same way as it was to their oral Word. That is, God (or Christ) is saying that His 'faithful and true' oral Word is extended to the written Word. 'Behold, I'm making all things new', and He said 'write this down for *these words are faithful and true*'.

So we see the extension of God's character, Christ's character, to His witness and oral Word in chapter 3. And now

John is commanded to write this word down in scriptural form in chapter 21. The faithful and true character of the oral Word is extended to the written form.

In 22:6 we see the same thing. We read, 'These words are faithful and true.' He is probably not just referring to the Revelation 21:1–22:5 vision but to the whole book. 'These words are faithful and true.' Again the whole book is categorized in this way. This is found in one other place. In 19:9 we read 'Then the angel said to me, "Write: 'Blessed are those who are invited to the wedding supper of the Lamb!'" And he added, "These are true words of God."' He is commanded to write. Why? Because what has been spoken as true has been extended to the written form. Only two verses later, Christ is again referred to as 'faithful and true'.

Now some might say, as they have in fact said to me, 'well there is a little room for slippage here. Yes, God is telling John to write these things down because the oral Word is "faithful and true," but maybe he could have slipped a little bit and just a bit of inaccuracy could have crept in when he tried to record it.' But, in fact, we know that John was a prophet, and we know that God views the whole book in its written form as prophetic. This is apparent from the well-known verses of Revelation 22:18-19, 'I warn everyone who hears the words of the prophecy of this book: If anyone adds to them, God will add to him the plagues which are written in this book. And if anyone takes away from the words of the book of this prophecy, God will take away his part from the tree of life.' And, likewise, remember that in chapter three, in the letters, at the end they are seen as the words of the Spirit, yet John was commanded to write.

So with this extension what we have here in Revelation is the syllogism. God and Christ are seen as faithful and true, therefore their oral Word is faithful and true, and because of this their Word is to be put down in written form, and this too is faithful and true. The word 'inerrant' is not used but certainly the notion is that God and Christ being 'faithful and true' includes that their witness not contain any untruth or error. Thus, the concept of inerrancy is likely expressed here.

DOWNES: What are some of the consequences of denying inerrancy?

BEALE: Ultimately, if you hold just to limited infallibility (for example, just the theological and soteric doctrines are inspired, not the other parts of the Bible), what can happen is that one ends up choosing what is inspired and trustworthy. What is infallible is different for different interpreters, and so one can end up making a Bible within the Bible for oneself. That is problematic. Someone might say that there are not a lot of errors, just a few. Well that is up to the 'error' decider. For some it may be more, for others less, but that way you don't end up with a fully inspired Bible.

I should address the typical objection that it is irrelevant to hold that the Scriptures were inspired in the original autographs, since we no longer have them. However, if we didn't have originally inspired autographs who knows how many errors we could have? And when did the Bible become inspired if they were not inspired in the originals? We are left with even more problems if we don't affirm a view of the inspiration of the original manuscripts. Furthermore, why do textual criticism if there was not an inspired original? Textual criticism is based on the fact that there was an original and that we are trying to get back to it.

Some people are concerned about the New Testament because there are corruptions in the manuscripts, which of course there are. But, in terms of the textual problems that we have, the really serious ones probably equal only one percent of the whole New Testament. Someone has compared this to the department of weights and measures in Washington D. C. Apparently, they have the perfect ruler there and the perfect foot. Carpenters around the country have rulers also. They are not as perfect as the one in Washington but they are very near it. To all intents and purposes we can say 'thus saith the Lord'.

If we are preaching from a text of which there is serious doubt about what the original said, then we have to acknowledge that, just as we have to acknowledge that there may be interpretative problems with some texts that maybe Augustine, Luther, Calvin and Hodge disagreed over. In fact, if we had the original autographs it wouldn't solve most of our problems. Most of our problems are theological and interpretive, not textual.

DOWNES: The doctrine of inerrancy has been criticized as "'practically worthless' because it requires so much qualifying. Andrew McGowan has recently questioned it on those grounds. Is it a fair criticism?

BEALE: You may be referring to his comments about the Chicago Statement on inerrancy. I do think it is important to make qualifications. All that is to say is that the Scripture is inerrant from the angle of God's intention through the human authors. If numbers are given in one text, and in parallel texts they are not exactly the same, is that an error? Well it depends on the intention of each particular author. One may be approximating and the other may not be. Some will say that is a qualification and that this qualification is a good example of inerrancy dying the death of a thousand qualifications. I don't think so.

Even those who hold to a broad view of inspiration, for example the infallibilists, will point to intention, even though they limit that intention to soteric issues or theological issues and not historical ones. I feel very happy with the qualifications that the Chicago Statement makes and I don't think that those qualifications qualify inerrancy in a way that it 'dies the death of a thousand qualifications'! In this connection, intriguingly, it is very striking, astonishing really, that Andrew McGowan's book has hardly any exegesis in it.

DOWNES: Another objection to inerrancy is that it is really a nineteenth-century invention that was forged in the conflict with liberal theology and higher criticism. How do you respond to that claim?

BEALE: What tells the tale on that are some of the articles and books that have been written that deal with the doctrine of Scripture in the apostolic fathers, the church fathers, the medieval period, the Reformation, and on up to the 1700s. The language used of Scripture throughout the history of the Church is the language of perfection, of not making mistakes, of not making errors and other synonymous terms. John Hannah has edited the book *Inerrancy and the Church*, in which there are several articles, beginning with the church fathers, that show that the doctrine of inerrancy is traceable long before the nineteenth century.

It is also a typical response to say that inerrancy arose from the Enlightenment, especially as this pertains to the use of reason in understanding Scripture. The response to this has to be the same as with the above discussion of the view of inspiration held throughout Church history.

DOWNES: What have been some of the contributing factors to what you have called the 'erosion' of inerrancy in evangelicalism?

BEALE: There are a number of factors. One has to do with the well-known term 'postmodernism'. What I mean by that term is the essential notion that truth is relative, and as that has come to be baptized within evangelicalism, especially in the United States, there is a focus away from the notion that the Scriptures are the inerrant Word of God and a focus on the Spirit coming to give every person a particular message through the Scriptures that may not have been originally intended. Hence, original inspiration is not that necessary or, at least, it comes to be seen as not so important.

Indeed, for the evangelical postmodernist, we no longer live in the former apologetic age. We live now in an age of experience where we want to meet the living God. We must not be so concerned about the inerrant propositions of Scripture.

'Propositions' almost has become a naughty hermeneutical word. We are told we should be concerned only with the God we meet who reveals His presence in Scripture. That is the kind of ethos that I think has worn away at the idea of inerrancy in evangelicalism.

Together with that there is another angle of the postmodern influence, and that is the notion that we moderns should not judge ancient peoples, i.e. the peoples who wrote the Bible, by our standards of what we believe is true and what is false. They may have had different standards. We should not impose our modern standards on these ancient peoples. For example, it is claimed that the synoptic gospels may indeed contain historical contradictions. That does not mean that the synoptic writers, and their readers, would have thought that they were contradictions and that they were false.

It is this kind of argument that you hear again and again, and this begins to touch even closer to the notion that truth is relative, especially from one age to another. That is one factor in the erosion of inerrancy in evangelicalism, even at some of our traditional evangelical institutions.

Secondly, there is a sociological phenomenon. Beginning at least thirty years ago, and increasingly today, evangelicals have been doing doctoral work in Old and New Testament and theology. One reason for that in Biblical Studies is that evangelical seminaries are rigorous in requiring Greek and Hebrew, whereas the other seminaries typically are not. There are more competent students potentially qualified to do doctoral work coming out of our seminaries (who know Greek and Hebrew well), and they are going on to do doctorates at non-evangelical institutions.

In the United States when one enters into a doctoral program that is not evangelical it is like entering a new world, a world that does not have the values that the student had back at their Christian college. When you go into that world as an evangelical you are made to feel like an ignorant fundamentalist if you really believe in the inspiration, indeed the inerrancy of Scripture. And if that were made known, you are then made to feel odd. No one wants to be made to feel odd by their professors and scholarly student peers. So it is very easy to downplay one's view, and it becomes very easy to want to fit in. In other words a student wants to be considered normal; no one wants to be seen as abnormal, and so there is tremendous pressure not to reveal one's belief in inerrancy, when particular occasions may call for it.

There is this huge sociological pressure placed on students, and if they are not tremendously founded on the Word of God and in a strong Reformed epistemology, then I have seen that it is easy for them to become conformed to that environment in which they are around. So students come out and maybe they are still evangelical, they believe in the gospel, but some of their other beliefs have been eroded, such as the full inspiration and inerrancy of Scripture, which they also begin to think is the fundamentalist view.

Those are two reasons for the erosion of inerrancy in evangelical: postmodern theological reasons and the sociological factors. I must say there are some students who go through these programs, and they do fine, but there is a significant percentage who come out still considering themselves as evangelical but not with the same set of beliefs on Scripture.

DOWNES: How do you assess the status of inerrancy today among evangelical theologians and biblical scholars? Is the doctrine in good health?

BEALE: Part of my answer goes back to the rise of postmodernism and its baptism into evangelicalism. You see this with some of our theologians at evangelical schools that do not want to be called systematic theologians. Systematic theology of some of these theologians is a matter of the past, a matter of Church history. Some contemporary theologians do not consider systematic theology to be a viable approach for the doing of theology today. These theologians sometimes like to refer to themselves as constructive theologians.

For them systematic theology focuses too much on reason, and the notion that you can organize Scripture into categories. They would also say that it focuses too much on propositions. So there is a de-emphasis on the inspiration of the propositions and an emphasis on the presence of God in Scripture. Of course that is a wonderful emphasis. Karl Barth had that emphasis. But you do not downplay one for the other. The propositions are true because they are living oracles of God and God is there speaking through them. The way He speaks to us existentially through the Scriptures is going to be consistent with the way they were originally penned under inspiration. There are not going to be different or contradictory meanings given by the Spirit.

I published a book in the mid 1990s called *The Right Doctrine from the Wrong Texts?* There is a debate still among evangelicals that the New Testament writers used the Old Testament but gave it *completely new meanings*, and yet what they wrote was inspired. I have to say 'no' to that. I have argued against that in a number of my writings and I think that is the opening of the door toward a dilution of inerrancy. Peter Enns, most recently of course, argued for this position in his book *Incarnation and Inspiration*.

Another symptom of the dilution of the authority of Scripture among evangelicals is the popularity of the Barthian view of Scripture. Of course, I don't want to paint everyone with this brush; there are some fine evangelicals upholding the doctrine of inerrancy, (and I'm not going to go school by school!), but some schools are mixed in this regard. I do think that the theology of Karl Barth's view of Scripture continues to live on, and in fact is becoming very, very much more influential, even more than it has been in the past, much more influential among evangelicals.

What that means is that the key issue is the presence of God confronting one in Scripture, and not so much the focus on propositions. Barth himself believed that there were actual errors in the inscripturated form of the Bible, but that God can reveal Himself even through those errors. This is a kind of strange hyper-Calvinist view. Some of these theologians would think that it is antiquated to try to defend inerrancy as an apologetic because of what they consider to be an appropriate lack of stress on propositions.

DOWNES: As a New Testament specialist what challenges have you faced in holding to an orthodox doctrine of Scripture?

BEALE: There are always passages that are very difficult, and one comes face to face with the question 'how do I handle this difficulty?' And what one does not want to do is to end up with bibliolatry, to turn the Bible into an idol. I think that can be done. You can have a wrong commitment to the Bible and its inerrancy if you come to a difficulty in the Bible and you press it down unnaturally, forcibly, to make it fit, to make it look like there is no problem in this text.

I think we need to be very honest and recognize that there are problems in the text and to let them stand. Our doctrine of inerrancy does not depend on our being able to solve every problem in the Bible, and in integrity we need to let them stand, and eventually, when we see the Lord, we will have the answers – not all of them of course. We have finite minds. God is infinite and He is the ultimate author of the Scriptures.

I think that some of the good work done in scholarship in the New Testament today is done by evangelicals because they have a high view of Scripture. They come to a difficulty and they are not willing to forcibly press it down. On the other hand they are not willing immediately in the same breath to say 'oh this is a mistake' which is the 'fundamentalist' liberal knee-jerk reaction. There are two fundamentalisms of course, liberal and conservative. And so some of these doctoral students and evangelical scholars will begin to do work on these difficult passages and do cutting edge work and solve some of them.

The reason I mention that in terms of my own experience is that there are problem texts I have come face to face with and I have to remember that I don't have to solve every problem there is in the Bible. I think one of the most difficult problems, for me, are the statements about the imminent coming of Christ. The scope of the biblical canon is also a very tough subject, though I believe the Protestant canon can be defended viably.

With regard to the imminence problem, there are texts in the gospels, and in Paul, which appear to say that there was a belief that Christ would come within the generation of the first century Christians. For example, in even another part of the New Testament, 1 John 2:18 says 'Dear children, this is the last hour; and as you have heard that the antichrist is coming, even now many antichrists have come. This is how we know it is the last hour.' As Raymond Brown in his commentary on 1 John said (which I paraphrase), 'I don't think it has been the last hour for two thousand years now.' He says that John was clearly wrong. At any rate, that is a difficulty. The latter days clearly began in the first century. Have the latter days really lasted two thousand years? That is one of the most difficult, pressing, problems for me as a New Testament theologian. But my answer to that last question is 'yes'.

The 'already and not yet' is a very important framework in eschatology, as well as the use that Paul makes of 'mystery' in Ephesians 3, and John in Revelation 10. Even Qumran used the word 'mystery' to affirm that the latter days were going to last a lot longer than it appeared from the Old Testament vantage point. I also think that the New Testament develops the idea that the Old Testament latter days will be fulfilled in a lot more drawn-out way. The parables in Matthew 13 of the mustard tree and the leaven speak to that to some degree as well.

So there are some tough texts and I realize that I have to think through them very carefully, but I don't have to solve every problem. And even with that most pressing problem that I mentioned about imminence, I think that there is an approach to that problem that is helpful (but there is not time to elaborate on that here).

DOWNES: What practical advice then would you give to evangelical students pursuing graduate Biblical Studies in secular university departments?

BEALE: If the student is not planning to try and teach at a high powered university in the United Kingdom or America but at an evangelical college or seminary then get your doctorate at a conservative place. There are some good programs out there: for example, at Wheaton, Trinity, Westminster Seminary or Dallas Theological Seminary. If one is thinking about going to a non-evangelical institution, it is my opinion that you need at least three if not four solid years at a masters level, studying exegesis, studying theology at an orthodox institution.

You need to have your beliefs really grounded. You need to know who you are, and why you are that way before you enter into an institution. It is a little bit tougher in the United States because you have to take more classes and so there is more of the professor's vantage points that a student is faced with. In the United Kingdom of course it is more of a research degree. The pressures are nevertheless comparable.

For someone who is already in a program, and of course it depends on what their background is, I think that one of the most important things is to be linked to the local church. Students tend to move from where they went to college to do doctoral work and so sometimes it might take a year to get settled into a church. That transitional year is very important, so really they need to get settled before that and they need to explore that before they move to a new town or country to start their doctoral programs. It is very important to be in a solid, orthodox evangelical church, and to stay close to the Lord in Scripture and prayer. If there are lingering or rising doubts about the Scriptures during research, then contact a scholar-pastor or biblical scholar or a theologian who is known to be orthodox, and get a good bibliography on the issues from both sides and work through it.

DOWNES: Do you think that evangelical scholars have underplayed the humanity of Scripture?

BEALE: There may be times when that is true, just as the humanity of Christ is underplayed sometimes. I want to be careful about making a sweeping deduction. You can have lay Christians who are very orthodox who may underplay the humanity of Scripture, but they may also underplay the humanity of Christ. This has been part of the reaction against the traditional view of inerrancy, but it is a not a problem, for example, with the view as it has been formulated in the Chicago Statement.

DOWNES: What are some of the essential books that pastors should be reading on the doctrine of Scripture?

BEALE: They should read the recent book *Ancient Word, Changing Worlds: The Doctrine of Scripture in a Modern Age* by Stephen Nichols and Eric Brandt. This is a historical overview of the orthodox view and elements of the erosion of the doctrine. I myself have taken up some case studies on various debates about inerrancy in *The Erosion of Inerrancy in Evangelicalism*.

Then there are some of the standard works. Of course, one has to first mention *The Inspiration and Authority of the Bible* by B. B. Warfield. Before reading anything else one must read that. And then I would add a very, very fine book by John Woodbridge which was an analysis back in the 1980s of the Rogers and McKim proposal on infallibility. That book is entitled *Biblical Authority*.

I want to go back to the 1950s and say that after Warfield, read J. I. Packer's little book *Fundamentalism and the Word of God*. This is a very fine book. I read it recently, after having thumbed through it for some years. I would also recommend

Inerrancy, edited by Norman Geisler. Other important books would be the two edited by D. A. Carson and John Woodbridge, *Scripture and Truth* and *Hermeneutics, Authority and Canon*. On the historical side I would recommend the previously mentioned *Inerrancy and the Church*, edited by John Hannah.

Chapter Twenty-Two

Being 'Against Heresies' is Not Enough

In Revelation 2 Jesus commends the church at Ephesus for their willingness to act in the face of error. They have shown discernment over the difference between true and false apostles, and having tested them they have actively rejected the false. Because of this they receive approving words from the glorified Son of God.

Whether or not churches today think this kind of discernment is a good thing is besides the point. Doubtless there is far too much confusion about the godliness, or not, of discernment, and far too much latitude when it comes to tolerating malevolent theologies.

It is possible to find ourselves clashing with Jesus because we weakly accept that He wants to be tested and rejected by churches. And of course the fact ought not to be lost on us that there are no false teachings, that are a clear and present danger to the churches, without there also being false teachers promoting them. Therefore there can be no exercise of discernment by churches without actively opposing those in error.

It is worth bearing in mind that there will be those who accept false teaching because they are sincerely ignorant, or guilty of sincere misinterpretation of what Scripture actually teaches. Damage is still inflicted on the church's health when this happens. The treatment for this is the persuasive power of the Word of God rightly understood. After all, isn't one of the functions of Scripture to correct as well as to teach?

Nonetheless not everyone proves responsive. Which is why Scripture specifies a fair hearing, a fair warning, and a fair rejection of a man who embraces error as spiritually aberrant in his message and his character. By testing, the church at Ephesus had found those who were rejects in the eyes of Jesus because they were 'false apostles'. This surely is good orthopraxy.

Whatever impression we have of these things among ourselves, which at times is as unsettling as watching the wind and the waves, we are called here to look upward to the assessment of Jesus. There may not be a place in our contemporary church culture and publications for the 'top 50 discerning churches', but these things do matter to the Son of God. We may not have peer approval, we may be frowned upon for an unloving stance, what does it matter though if He approves of us?

Jesus commends discernment. That is of great worth to churches seeking to honor His truth. If you find yourself in this situation it will put strength and heart into you to know that you have His approval. As Bonar put it:

> Men heed thee, love thee, praise thee not;
> The Master praises: what are men?

Not only is this so, but the church at Ephesus is also found to be persevering, hard working, willing to endure for Christ's name, and all without weariness. In a culture of ease and compromise here are dimensions of church life the very existence of which we ought to be deeply thankful for.

But it is not enough. Being discerning is not enough. Being against heresies is not enough. Being hardworking, persevering, and enduring is not enough. Even such commendable churches can be doomed. Even they can find that Jesus is going to bring them to an end. Such churches can have lost their first love.

Don Carson summarizes this so well:

> If this church does not repent, it is doomed. The destruction might take two or three generations; it might take longer. But sooner or later the candlestick is removed; sooner or later the church that no longer finds obedience to the first and second great commandments a delight is sinking into the mire of idolatry and self-love--regardless of how orthodox, active, and zealous it is.
>
> Here is our first duty, our fundamental privilege, our basic worship: to love God with heart and soul and mind and strength, and our neighbor as ourselves. In the midst of suffering, persecution, disability, disappointment, infirmity, tiredness, duty, discipline, work, witness, discernment-- in short in the midst of everything--that love remains our first duty, our fundamental privilege, our basic worship still.
>
> When we grow old and calamitously weak, we must love God still; when we look after the chronically ill and think that our horizons are shriveling up, we must love God still; when we are bereaved, we must love God still; when we study and work and build and witness, we must love God still; when we exercise theological discernment, we must love God still. And still, too, must we love our neighbor as ourselves.
>
> So we have returned to love in hard places, the first of the hard places--the hard places of our own hearts, our own souls.

> D. A. Carson, *Love in Hard Places*, p. 185-6

CHAPTER TWENTY-THREE

CLEAR AND PRESENT DANGER

Reflections on Dealing With False Teaching and Teachers in 1 Timothy

---

This chapter is an expanded version of an article, 'Clear and Present Danger: Timothy and the False Teachers', which appeared in *The Banner of Truth* magazine, August/September 2006, No. 515-6, reprinted with permission.

In this concluding chapter I want to reflect a little on the backdrop of false teaching in 1 Timothy and on Paul's response to it. What follows is not intended to be an exegetical commentary, or to provide a reconstruction of the social and religious background of the Ephesian church. On these matters readers should consult *Letters and Homilies for Hellenized Christians Volume 1* by Ben Witherington and *The Pastoral Epistles: A Commentary on the Greek Text* by George W. Knight. Rather, I want to draw some general directives, some big picture applications, to the shape and texture of pastoral ministry and church life today.

There is a book in my study that is the spiritual equivalent of arsenic or cyanide. If it was in liquid form it would be in a bottle with an orange hazard label on the side. It is the most dangerous book that I own. It is so dangerous that early on in the seventeenth century it was publicly burned by order of the English Parliament. It is called the *Racovian Catechism*.

The *Racovian Catechism* specifically denies and attacks the doctrine of the Trinity, the deity of Jesus Christ, and the nature of His atoning death as both penal and substitutionary. In comparison to many other books that attack penal substitution it is perhaps the gold standard. And a copy of it sits on my bookshelf in the church where I pastor. Can it do people any harm? Well, the answer is yes and no. The answer is 'no' if it sits on my shelf rather innocuously gathering dust. But of course if someone were to read it, become persuaded by its arguments, and then seek to convince others to accept them, the situation would be rather different. From being dormant it will have become a 'clear and present danger.' And all because its ideas had found an advocate.

There were people like that in first century Ephesus. I don't mean to suggest that they were the early ancestors of the Socinians, but rather that the Ephesian church was troubled by active proponents of gospel denying error. They, as well as their teaching, needed to be dealt with. It is not just the content of their teaching that concerned Paul. These false teachers had corrupt characters to match their teaching. People were promoting these ideas, and they must be stopped. This is what Timothy has been charged to do (1 Tim. 1:3-4). Having swerved away from the truth that leads to godly living they had wandered away into vain discussion (1 Tim. 1:5-7). Paul's point is that you cannot deal with the spread of false teaching without engaging, in one way or another, with false teachers.

General features of error

James Buchanan wrote some very wise words about truth and error in his classic work *The Doctrine of Justification*:

> It has long been my firm conviction, that the only effective refutation of error is the establishment of

> truth. Truth is one, error is multiform; and truth, once firmly established, overthrows all the errors that either have been, or may yet be, opposed to it. He who exposes and expels an error, does well; but it will only return in another form, unless the truth has been so lodged in the heart as to shut it out for ever.

Errors are of course specific. Timothy has to deal with specific distortions, denials and differences in doctrine that we will not be dealing with in an identical way today. That said, there are some generic features of the false teaching found here that every age has to deal with. Paul refers to these errors as 'different' doctrine. Different from what? From the apostolic gospel, from 'the faith,' from the 'sound words of the Lord Jesus Christ and the teaching that accords with godliness' (6:3). So this teaching is different in its nature, content, and effects, to the apostolic gospel. Like the Galatians they were being presented with a different gospel (Gal. 1:6).

This choice of different doctrine involved two things. It denied the true gospel, and in its place, promoted a different one. It was of sufficient seriousness to change the content of saving Christian truth and to overturn the unity and peace of the church (2 Tim. 2:18; Titus 1:11).

It would be a mistake to think that all errors are equally heinous. Every error in doctrine leads to undesirable pastoral consequences. Believing them will lead us to think, live and worship in a distorted way. The last two hundred years give ample evidence of this concerning the doctrine of sanctification. Well meaning Christians have tried to live holy lives based on ideas that are not biblical (Higher Life, 'let Go and let God', and various forms of perfectionism). Here are errors that call for correction and clear teaching. These ideas were at times promoted by preachers who were unsaved. They were also promoted by preachers who were saved but badly mistaken. But Timothy has to deal with errors of a greater magnitude, errors that change the very nature and content of the gospel message.

There are two generic features of the false teaching that forms the backdrop to 1 Timothy:

i. There are errors connected with revelation.
There are 'myths' and 'genealogies'. By myth Paul means an unreal tale that only the gullible believe. Extra-biblical revelation is in view here. Whatever these myths were about, the issue at stake is plain. Where does the authority lie? Where does the buck stop in the realm of ideas? Made up stories and human imagination or the Word of God? They stand in direct contrast to the knowledge of the truth in the apostolic gospel (2:4-7).

It is clear that the Word is not sufficient for these teachers, they have turned away from it in preference for legends. There is clear rejection of the truth, and error fills the gap that is left. As one man put it, our response to revelation is either the 'bowed head or turned back'.

ii. There are errors of interpretation.
They are ignorant about the relationship of the law and the gospel (1:7-10). They don't understand that the law's primary function is to expose sin and not to produce speculative legalists. Dealing with errors in interpretation, both sincere and sinful, will be the kind of thing that pastors encounter all the time. It seems that Paul is dealing with sincere misinterpretation in 1 Corinthians 5:9-11. However, the accompanying feature of a wrong interpretation of the law in 1 Timothy is the loss of a good conscience. These false teachers have moved away from purity of heart and sincerity of faith. They are not sincere in their misunderstanding, the kind of people that need to be gently taught and shown the right way. No, they are sinful and wilful in their misunderstanding, having wandered away from the truth.

Is it true that at the micro level our exegesis is always 100% correct? No preacher would claim that. But Paul has in mind here the macro level, the very structure of redemptive revelation. These enthusiastic teachers of the law are devoid of understanding (1:8), they don't know what they are talking about. The lawful use of the law is to expose sin. In this the law and the gospel agree. It is possible to hold to *sola scriptura* but to end up in gross error when it coms to interpreting the Bible. The false teachers in Ephesus, it seems, were guilty of both errors. They added to Scripture and destructively confused law and gospel.

Error and the staple diet of churches
Paul's concern was not so much to extensively describe the false teaching but to charge Timothy to stop the false teachers teaching it. His language shows his mind on it. Paul is scornful. The genealogies are endless! Gallons of ink has been spilled in the effort to work out what these errors were. Paul, it seems, is content with minimum reportage for either Timothy is very familiar with them or else his attention is being directed elsewhere. Titus received similar advise; these things were foolish, unprofitable and worthless (Titus 3:9).

The *Westminster Directory of Public Worship* has a striking comment on how a preacher should deal with false doctrine:

> In confutation of false doctrines, he is neither to raise an old heresy from the grave, nor to mention a blasphemous opinion unnecessarily: but, if the people be in danger of an error, he is to confute it soundly, and endeavor to satisfy their judgements and consciences against all objections.

Timothy's ministry is to be essentially positive. He is to en-sure right doctrine and conduct in God's household (3:14-16), devoting himself to the public reading of Scripture, teaching and exhortation (4:6, 11, 13). He must deal with the clear and present danger that the people are in. But when they are not in danger why trouble them with things that are unprofitable?

Archibald Alexander gave shrewd counsel to pastors on this point. His words should be carefully weighed as well as read:

> The truth has its best effect when it is proposed simply and unconnected with false opinions which may be entertained by some. It is but to hold forth the word of life as true and certain, as if it had never been controverted. Preachers who are forever brandishing the polemical sword may make their hearers skilful in controversy, and they will be sure to catch the spirit of polemics too. But what they gain in acuteness of intellect and keenness of temper, they will lose in improvement of heart.
>
> Men may be forever considering the truth as it comes up in controversy, and never be affected with its beauty and force.
>
> I do not mean to say that a minister of the gospel must never resort to controversy. I would say on this subject as on that of war; it is a necessary evil. We should never engage in it unless it is forced on us, and then kick it out of the pulpit if possible.
>
> When controversy is forced upon you by the perverseness, pride or obstinacy of others see that you contend only with gospel weapons ... You are commanded to instruct those who oppose you with meekness. Severity may be used when the evil will not yield to mild admonition and gentle persuasion – but it should not be the severity of sinful resentment, but of holy zeal for the honor of God's truth.

Buchanan, the *Directory*, and Alexander all caution us to shape Christian ministry by the positive truths of the gospel. This is the pattern laid down by Paul and that must continue to mould pastoral ministry today.

False teaching and morality

Sound doctrine leads to sound living. The gospel promotes godliness. Ungodly behavior is the natural outworking of doctrines that are not true. They promote speculations and vain discussion, not love that issues from a pure heart, a good conscience and a sincere faith (1:5-6). Let go of faith and a good conscience and you will be shipwrecked like Hymenaeus and Alexander (1:19-20; 2 Tim. 2:16-18). Depart from the 'faith' and you will end up with deceitful spirits and demonic doctrines, and the insincerity of liars with seared consciences whose moral teaching contradicts the Word of God (4:1-5).

Paul paints an ugly portrait of the moral and spiritual condition of a false teacher at the close of the letter:

> He is puffed up with conceit and understands nothing. He has an unhealthy craving for controversy and for quarrels about words, which produce envy, dissension, slander, evil suspicions, and constant friction among people who are depraved in mind and deprived of the truth (6:4-5, esv).

Their teaching was shown to be false by its practical outcome. They were known by their fruit (Matt. 7:20). G. K. Chesterton was right on target when he wrote that 'heresy always affects morality, if it's heretical enough.'

The end result of this teaching interests Paul. It is speculation and dispute. The very content and nature of this teaching fails to promote what the apostolic gospel promotes. Calvin's letter to Laelio Socinus (the uncle of Faustus, the heretical genius behind the *Racovian Catechism*) is worth pondering:

> Certainly no one can be more averse to paradox than I am, and in subtleties I find no delight at all. Yet nothing shall ever hinder me from openly avowing what I have learned from the Word of God; for nothing but what is useful is taught in the school of this master. It is my only guide, and

to acquiesce in its plain doctrines shall be my constant rule of wisdom.

Would that you also, my dear Laelius, would learn to regulate your powers with the same moderation! You have no reason to expect a reply from me so long as you bring forward those monstrous questions. If you are gratified by floating among those airy speculations, permit me, I beseech you, an humble disciple of Christ, to meditate on those things which tend towards the building up of my faith.

... And in truth I am very greatly grieved that the fine talents with which God has endowed you, should be occupied not only with what is vain and fruitless, but that they should also be injured by pernicious figments.

What I warned you of long ago, I must again seriously repeat, that unless you correct in time this itching after investigation, it is to be feared you will bring upon yourself severe suffering.

But Laelio's ears were deaf as well as itching. Having wandered away from the truth he ended up by fostering a movement that denied virtually every distinctively Christian doctrine.

What is sometimes lost sight of today is that as well as leading to ungodliness and immorality, there is also a moral dimension to the very unwillingness to receive and continue in the truth of the gospel. This connection was, however, noted in by the early church fathers. Jaroslav Pelikan observed that:

Heresy was treated by the early church as the concern not only of doctrinal theology, but also of moral theology, of canon law, and finally of civil law as well. This was not only because of the stock accusation that false doctrine led to 'all those kinds of forbidden deeds of which the Scriptures assure us that 'they who do such things shall not inherit

244

the kingdom of God,' but because of the claim
that the invention and especially the propagation
of false doctrine were due to a vainglory that has
preoccupied their mind' (Irenaeus).

Drawing some conclusions for today

Ministers must be polemical in their public teaching when
they need to be, but not otherwise. In the course of expounding passages dealing with these matters, and when there is
real threat. In their private study there is of course need to
be aware of men and movements that are dangerous. Those
training for ministry and Christian service ought to be
familiar with contemporary and historical examples of denials and distortions of Christian doctrine. This is not an appeal for ignorance or dropping our guard.

Congregations should be spared from hearing about the
specific details of false teaching unless it is absolutely necessary.
There are winds of doctrine in the evangelical world, but are
they affecting us? Should we not concentrate on things that
are? If false teaching is unprofitable and worthless what good
can come from considering it? Should we not look at our
own sins and situations and address those issues instead?

We should concentrate on the positive upbuilding of the
church. There is work enough here. The rest of 1 Timothy
expands on this. If truth is one, more is gained by the positive
exposition of the truth than by detailing the multiple forms
of error. Are we teaching the whole counsel of God? Are we
ensuring that people are well grounded in essential biblical
doctrines and shown how to rightly interpret Scripture? Do
we share Paul's pastoral heart and aims found in Col. 1:28-29?
Don't waste time on matters that are not a threat to your
situation. The time is short. Is that not how Nehemiah treated
his opponents? Put good things before the church and have
nothing to do with silly, irreverent myths (4:6-7).

Preachers need to guard their hearts and their ministry.
As Francis Schaeffer once wrote, reflecting on the battle for

the gospel in the 1930s, 'be careful what habits you pick up in controversy.' A polemical ministry is necessary. We must contend for the faith. But we must guard against a contentious spirit. Preoccupation with error is not good for the minister or the church. This is Paul's charge to Titus. The gospel of salvation is excellent for people, the root of faith promotes the fruit of good works. This is profitable. But these other teachings are unprofitable and useless. Avoid them, they thrive in an atmosphere of contention (Titus 3:9-11).

The great John Owen wrote a massive scholarly refutation of the errors found in the *Racovian Catechism* with the Latin title *Vindicae Evangelicae*. In the penultimate section of his introduction, he addressed the vital necessity of knowing the power of the truth in our own experience. That he should write like this at the beginning of a sharply polemical book models for us what must be at the heart of contending for the faith in a way that pleases God:

> When the heart is cast indeed into the mould of the doctrine that the mind embraceth; when the evidence and necessity of the truth abides in us; when not the sense of the words only is in our heads, but the sense of the things abides in our hearts; when we have communion with God in the doctrine we contend for – then shall we be garrisoned, by the grace of God, against all the assaults of men. And without this all our contending is, as to ourselves, of no value.
>
> What am I the better if I can dispute that Christ is God, but have no sense or sweetness in my heart from hence that He is a God in covenant with my soul?
>
> What will it avail me to evince by testimonies and arguments, that He hath made satisfaction for sin if, through my unbelief, the wrath of God abideth on me, and I have no experience of my

own being made the righteousness of God in him,--if I find not, in my standing before God, the excellency of having my sins imputed to Him and His righteousness imputed to me?

Will it be any advantage to me, in the issue, to profess and dispute that God works the conversion of a sinner by the irresistible grace of His Spirit, if I was never acquainted experimentally with the deadness and utter impotency to good, that opposition to the law of God, which is in my own soul by nature, with the efficacy of the exceeding greatness of the power of God in quickening, enlightening, and bringing forth the fruits of obedience in me?

It is the power of truth in the heart alone that will make us cleave unto it indeed in an hour of temptation.

Let us, then, not think that we are any thing the better for our conviction of the truths of the great doctrines of the gospel, for which we contend with these men, unless we find the power of the truths abiding in out own hearts, and have a continual experience of their necessity and excellency in our standing before God and our communion with Him.

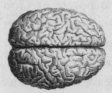

*Fig.1 The Christian Mind
(Endangered)*

EVANGELICAL
CONCERNS

Rediscovering the Christian mind
on issues facing the Church today

*"The intelligence, breadth of learning, and
readability offer important and timely lessons."*

Professor Paul Helm
King's College, London

MELVIN TINKER

ISBN 978-1-85792-675-0

Evangelical Concerns

Rediscovering the Christian Mind on Issues Facing the Church Today

MELVIN TINKER

We are sometimes left with the feeling that evangelicals stand in the shadows of a collapsing culture with nothing but two alternatives open to us: either to retreat into a ghetto or sell out on fundamental issues of truth. Here, Melvin Tinker suggests a 'Third Way' – to develop a fully orbed biblical approach to science and socio-political issues – and so to regain the Christian mind.

> If you lap up Francis Schaeffer, Os Guiness and David Wells, you will enjoy this – and find yourself agreeing with most of it.
>
> Jonathan Stephen,
> Wales Evangelical School of Theology

> The intelligence, breadth of learning, and readability offer important and timely lessons.
>
> Paul Helm,
> Regent College, Vancouver, Canada

Melvin Tinker is Vicar of St John's Newland, Chairman of Yorkshire Gospel Partnership, Co-director of Northern Training Course and is a leading member of the Anglican group 'REFORM'.

HEROES&
HERETICS

PIVOTAL MOMENTS IN 20 CENTURIES OF THE CHURCH

IAIN D. CAMPBELL

ISBN 978-1-85792-925-6

Heroes & Heretics

Pivotal Moments on the 20 Centuries of Church

IAIN D. CAMPBELL

Iain D. Campbell has set out a lively and absorbing summary of history, one century at a time. The result entices you into the great sweeping themes of history that show God at work through his church.

> ... a wise and breathtaking panorama of almost two thousand years of the history of the church with observations and insights in every single chapter.
>
> Geoffrey Thomas

> 'In an age where Christians are increasingly ignor-ant of their historical roots, Dr Campbell has done us a great service by achieving the near impossible: covering 2000 years of church history in twenty brief but highly informative chapters. A great place to start for anyone who wants to deepen their understanding of how the church has witnessed to Christ throughout the ages.'
>
> Carl Trueman,
> Westminster Theological Seminary, Philadelphia

Rev. Dr. Iain D. Campbell is pastor of the Free Church of Scotland in Back on the Isle of Lewis. His previous books include *The Doctrine of Sin* (ISBN 978-1-85792-438-1) and *Heart of the Gospel* (ISBN 978-1-85792-182-3). He is also the Review Editor of the *Scottish Bulletin of Evangelical Theology*.

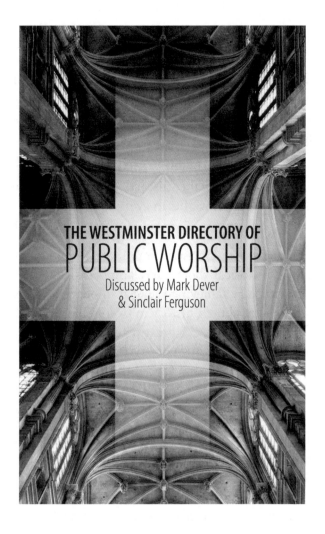

THE WESTMINSTER DIRECTORY OF
PUBLIC WORSHIP
Discussed by Mark Dever
& Sinclair Ferguson

ISBN 978-1-84550-427-4

The Westminster Directory of Public Worship

DISCUSSED BY

MARK DEVER & SINCLAIR B. FERGUSON

The Directory of Public Worship was composed by the same group who wrote the Westminster Confession of Faith and the Larger and Shorter Catechisms. They were appointed by the British parliament to restructure the Church of England. These documents form the basis of the Presbyterian system of church government and practice. Here it is discussed by Sinclair Ferguson and Mark Dever. They write with clarity making it palatable even to modern readers beset by busyness & multiple distractions.

> *The Directory's* outline of what is involved in the exposition of Scripture could fruitfully be engraved onto the desk of every preacher of the gospel. Wisely their instruction was framed in a way that made it applicable to a whole range of preaching methods and styles ...
>
> Sinclair B. Ferguson

> *The Westminster Directory of Public Worship* represents a flowering of Puritan understanding on topics such as the public reading of scripture, public prayer, and the preaching of the Word. The best way to introduce you to the Puritans' thinking is to urge you to read [*The Westminster Directory of Public Worship*] ... in which the Puritans speak for themselves.
>
> Mark Dever

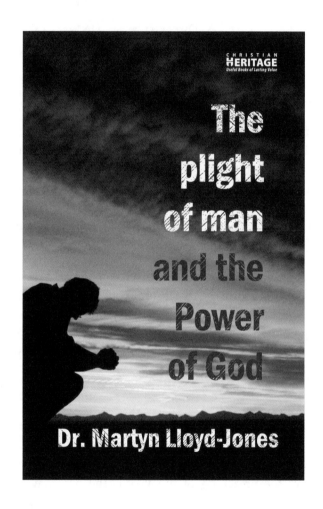

ISBN 978-1-84550-439-7

The Plight of Man and the Power of God

Dr Martyn Lloyd-Jones

> We must rouse ourselves and realize afresh that though our Gospel is timeless and changeless, it nevertheless is always contemporary. We must meet the present situation and we must speak a word to the world that none else can speak.
>
> Martyn Lloyd-Jones

This author's preaching always had an emphasis on the desperate plight of man and the power of God to save. His preaching was crystal clear on the sovereignty of God in the salvation of sinners, a concept that does not sit comfortably in our day of pragmatism, programs and self-help books. Nevertheless it remains at the core of what the world needs to hear. Based on the Romans 1, this wonderful book will help you understand what the gospel is. When we live in a world that is spiralling out of control we will want to hear this message again and again.

Dr Martyn Lloyd-Jones (1899–1981) was born in Wales and at the age of 27 gave up a most promising medical career to become a preacher. When a spiritual history of the 20th century comes to be written it will include not only the far-reaching influence of Dr. Lloyd Jones' ministry at Westminster Chapel in London from 1938-68, but also the remarkable fact that his published volumes of expository sermons have had an unprecedented circulation, selling millions of copies.

Christian Focus Publications

publishes books for all ages
Our mission statement –

STAYING FAITHFUL
In dependence upon God we seek to help make His infallible
Word, the Bible, relevant. Our aim is to ensure that the Lord
Jesus Christ is presented as the only hope to obtain forgiveness
of sin, live a useful life and look forward to heaven with Him.

REACHING OUT
Christ's last command requires us to reach out to our world
with His gospel. We seek to help fulfil that by publishing
books that point people towards Jesus and help them develop
a Christ-like maturity. We aim to equip all levels of readers
for life, work, ministry and mission.

Books in our adult range are published in three imprints.
Christian Focus contains popular works including bio-
graphies, commentaries, basic doctrine and Christian living.
Our children's books are also published in this imprint.
Mentor focuses on books written at a level suitable for Bible
College and seminary students, pastors, and other serious
readers. The imprint includes commentaries, doctrinal
studies, examination of current issues and church history.
Christian Heritage contains classic writings from the past.

Christian Focus Publications Ltd
Geanies House, Fearn, Ross-shire,
IV20 1TW, Scotland, United Kingdom
info@christianfocus.com
www.christianfocus.com